The Best of Guideposts® CHRISTMAS

The Best of
Guideposts.
CHRISTMAS

A COLLECTION OF CHRISTMAS STORIES
FROM AMERICA'S FAVORITE MAGAZINE

Ideals Publications
Nashville, Tennessee

ISBN 0-8249-4645-6

Published by Ideals Publications
A division of Guideposts
535 Metroplex Drive, Suite 250
Nashville, Tennessee 37211
www.idealsbooks.com

Publisher, Patricia A. Pingry
Editor, Peggy Schaefer
Designer, Marisa Calvin
Copy Editor, Melinda Rathjen
Cover photograph, Taxi/Getty Images

Library of Congress Cataloging-in-Publication Data

The best of Guideposts : Christmas : a collection of Christmas stories from
America's favorite magazine.
     p. cm.
  Includes index.
  ISBN 0-8249-4645-6 (alk. paper)
  1. Christmas—Miscellanea. I. Guideposts (Pawling, N.Y.)
  BV45.B47 2005
  242'.335—dc22

                              2005010914

Printed and bound in Italy by LEGO
10 9 8 7 6 5 4 3 2 1

ACKNOWLEDGMENTS
"The Night the Stars Sang" originally appeared in *Nothing Ever Happens and
How It Does* by Dorothy Canfield Fisher. Published in 1940 by Beacon Press,
Boston. Reprinted in *Guideposts* magazine December 1959.
       All other stories originally appeared in *Guideposts* magazine and are
copyright © by Guideposts, Carmel, New York 10512. All rights reserved.

* A Mediamark Research Inc. study in fall 2004 asked readers of 206 major
magazines to name their favorites. *Guideposts* ranked number one among all
adults and among women.

Contents

Foreword

CHRISTMAS IS ALL ABOUT A STORY, the story of a baby born to humble parents in a tiny Bethlehem stable under a brilliant eastern star—a story that changed the world forever. So it comes as no surprise that some of *Guideposts* magazine's greatest stories are about Christmas, and how people are inspired and lives are changed at this blessed time of year. For there is a resonance from that birth that echoes through time and through our very hearts. Every story in this collection is proof of the enduring power of that first Christmas, true personal accounts of transformation told by ordinary people . . . and not-so-ordinary people. You will read about blessings, traditions, forgiveness, love, faith, giving, miracles, and angels. All the themes that make this season truly holy.

Have you ever felt lonely at Christmas? Widower Jimmy Gupton did, until he took in a struggling young married couple with a baby on the way. Jimmy learned that there is always room at the inn, and always a reason to go on living.

A copywriter who yearns to give gifts that really mean something has her prayer answered in a way she could have never imagined. A single mom struggling to raise two young daughters discovers the power of a puppy to soothe hurting hearts. A firefighter's vivid and disturbing dream saves a family from death on Christmas Eve.

Then there is the account of a mysterious disappearance of the Christ Child from the manger scene at Victory Church. Who could have done such a thing? You'll be surprised to find out. I was. Almost as surprised as I was to learn how writer Kitty Slattery's missing tooth led her to a deeper understanding of the Christmas spirit.

There are familiar names too. Hollywood legend Jimmy Stewart will tell you why it really is "a wonderful life" and what that classic holiday movie meant to him on the most personal level. Celebrated ornament-maker Christopher Radko introduces you to his Polish grandmother and explains how the desire not to disappoint her led him to design his first beautiful creations. Beloved actor Michael Landon talks about the angels in his life, human and otherwise.

My favorite holiday stories, though, come from our "His Mysterious Ways" feature—year in and year out the most popular page in the magazine. Here you will meet people from all walks of life who have experienced something inexplicable, even miraculous, at Christmastime—incredible stories that will send a shiver down your spine and warm your heart as well.

This book is filled with stories you will never forget from the little magazine that has inspired millions of readers for sixty years. So go ahead, start reading, and find out why *Guideposts* is America's favorite magazine, especially at Christmas.

—Edward Grinnan, Editor-in-Chief, *Guideposts*

Blessings at Christmastime

The Night the Stars Sang

Dorothy Canfield Fisher

December 1959

At odd, quiet hours in her day, almost every mother wonders about her child's immortal soul. Will it emerge from the little ragamuffin who has just left his wet lollipop on the davenport? When will the person inside come to the surface? Will anyone be there to see, and to wonder?

I know a mother who was there, who did see, and who did wonder. She told me about it, and I don't think she will mind if I tell you. It all began a few weeks before Christmas.

"Well," she said cheerily one afternoon to David, her eight-year-old, and two of his friends, "what Christmas songs are you learning in your classroom this year?"

Looking down at his feet, David answered sadly, "Teacher says we can't sing good enough. She's only going to let kids sing in the entertainment who can carry a tune."

Inwardly the mother broke into a mother's rage at the teacher. *So that's what she says, does she? What's she for, if not to teach children what they don't know?*

She drew in a deep breath, then said quietly, "Well, how'd you like to practice your song with me?"

Together the four went into the living room to the piano. "What song is your class to sing?"

"It came upon the midnight—" said the three boys, speaking at once.

"That's a nice one," she commented, reaching for the battered songbook on top of the piano. "This is the way it goes." She played the air and sang the first two lines.

They opened their mouths and sang out lustily: "It came upon the midnight clear, that glorious song of old. . . ."

At the end of that phrase, David's mother stopped abruptly, and for an instant bowed her head over the keys. Her feeling about the teacher made a right-about turn.

She finally lifted her head and turned a smiling face on the three waiting children. "I tell you what," she said, "the way, really, to learn a tune is just one note after another. I'll strike just the two first notes on the piano: 'It came—'" Full of goodwill, the little boys sang with her.

She stopped and breathed hard.

"Not quite," she said with a false smile, "Pretty good. I think we'd better take it one note at a time. Bill, you try it."

After a pause she said, "Peter, it's your turn."

That evening, after the children had gone to bed, she told her husband, "You never heard anything like that in your whole life, Harry—never. You can't imagine what it was like!"

"Oh, yes I can too," he said over his temporarily lowered

newspaper. "I've heard plenty of tone-deaf kids hollering. I know what they sound like. There are people, you know, who really can't carry a tune."

Seeing, perhaps, in her face, the mulish mother-stubbornness, he added, with a little exasperation, "What's the use of trying to do what you can't do?"

That was reasonable, she thought. But the next morning, when she was downtown, she turned in at the public library and picked up two books on teaching music to children.

During the weeks between then and the Christmas entertainment, the mother didn't see how she could ever keep it up. She discovered, to her dismay, that the little boys had no idea whether a note was higher or lower than the one before it.

She adapted and invented "musical games" to train their ears for this. Standing in a row, their backs to the piano, listening to decide whether the second note was "uphill or downhill" from the first note, the boys thought it as good a game as any other. They laughed raucously over each other's mistakes, ran a contest to see who came out best.

There were times when the mother faltered—many times. When she saw the ironing heaped high, or when her daughter, Janey, was in bed with a cold, she would say to herself, *Today I'll just tell the boys that I cannot go on with this. We're not getting anywhere, anyhow.*

Then she would remember that Christmas celebrated the birth of the Savior—and that one of Christ's most beloved traits was patience.

So when the boys came storming in, certain that she would

not close that door she had half-opened for them, she laid everything aside and went to the piano.

As a matter of fact, they were getting somewhere. Even with their backs to the piano, the boys could now tell, infallibly, whether a second note was above or below the first one. About the second week of December, they could all sound—if they remembered to sing softly and to listen to themselves—a note, any note, within their range, she struck on the piano.

After that it went fast—the practicing of the song, repeating it for the at-first skeptical and then thoroughly astonished teacher, and then reporting triumphantly at home, "Teacher says we can sing it good enough. She says we can sing with the others. We practiced going up on the platform this afternoon."

Then came the day of the Christmas entertainment. Boys clomped up the aisle; girls swished their short skirts proudly. David's mother clutched her handbag nervously.

The crash from the piano gave them the tone; all the mouths opened and began, "It came upo-on the midnight clear, that glorious so-ong of old. . . ."

The mother's tense hands relaxed. The teacher's long drills and her own hard work had been successful. It was not howling; it was singing. There were swelling crescendos; and at the lines, "The world in so-olemn stillness lay to hear the a-angels sing. . . ." the child voices were hushed in a diminuendo. Part of the mother's very life, she thought wryly, had been spent in securing her part of the diminuendo.

So there he stood, her little David, a fully accredited part of his corner of society, as good as anybody, the threat of the inferiority feeling averted this time. The door had been slammed in his face. She had pushed it open, and he had gone through.

The hymn ended. The burst of parental applause began clamorously. The third grade filed down from the platform. Surely, now, the mother thought, David would turn his head to where she sat and thank her with a look. Just this once.

He did turn his head as he filed by. He looked fully at his family—at his father, his mother, his kid sister, his big brother, and his sister from the high school. He gave them a formal, small nod to acknowledge publicly that they were his family. But his mother knew that his look was not for her alone. It was just as much for those of his family who had been bored and impatient spectators of her struggle to help him, as for her who had given part of her life to roll that stone uphill.

She sighed. Mothers were to accept what they received, without bitterness, without resentment. After all, that was what mothers worked for—not for thanks, but to do their job. The sharp chisel of life, driven home by experience, flaked off expertly another flint-hard chip from her blithe, selfish girlhood. It fell away from the woman she was growing to be, and dropped soundlessly into the abyss of time.

But a few nights later, close to Christmas, the mother looked out her kitchen window to see if David was returning from a neighbor's. The night was cloudless, cold, and still. Her backyard was almost transparent in the pale radiance that fell from the stars.

Then she saw David. Knee-deep in the snow, he stood looking all around him. Then he lifted his face towards the sky. What could he be looking at? Or hearing?

She opened the kitchen door and stepped out into the dark, under the stars. He came quickly to her and put his arms around her. With every fiber of her body which had borne his, she felt a difference in him.

"It's so still," he said quietly in a hushed voice, a voice she had never heard before.

"All those stars," he murmured dreamily, "they shine so. But they don't make a sound."

He stood a little away from her to look up into her face. "Do you remember—in the song—'the world in solemn stillness lay'?"

The starlight illumined him clearly, his honest, little-boy eyes wide, fixed trustingly on his mother's, and in them she saw the miracle—the miracle of an awakening soul.

He had not known that he had an inner sanctuary. Now he stood in it, awe-struck at his first sight of beauty, and opened the door to his mother.

As naturally as he breathed, he put into her hands the pure rounded pearl of a shared joy.

"I thought I heard them singing—sort of," he whispered.

I Remember
Three Christmases

Norman Vincent Peale

December 1974

So it comes again, this marvelous Christmas season, the time of chimes and carols, of joy and wonder. A time of fond memories too, when people look back with love and longing to other Christmases.

There are three particular Christmases in my own past that had a special warmth for me. As everyone knows, gold and frankincense and myrrh were the first Christmas offerings. The gifts given to me on those three occasions were invisible, but they were no less real. Each came unexpectedly—and each left me a changed person.

I

Some of my most impressionable boyhood years were spent in Cincinnati. I still remember the huge Christmas tree in Fountain Square—the gleaming decorations, the streets ringing with the sound of carols. Up on East Liberty Street, where we lived, my mother always had a Christmas tree with real candles on it, magical candles which, combined with the fir tree, gave off a foresty aroma, unique and unforgettable.

One Christmas Eve, when I was twelve, I was out with my father, a minister, doing some late Christmas shopping. He had me loaded down with packages and I was tired and cross. I was thinking how good it would be to get home when a beggar—a bleary-eyed, unshaven, dirty old man—came up to me, touched my arm with a hand like a claw, and asked for money. He was so repulsive that instinctively I recoiled.

Softly my father said, "Norman, it's Christmas Eve. You shouldn't treat a man that way."

I was unrepentant. "Dad," I said, "he's nothing but a bum."

My father stopped. "Maybe he hasn't made much of himself, but he's still a child of God." He then handed me a dollar—a lot of money for those days and for a preacher's income. "I want you to take this and give it to that man," he said. "Speak to him respectfully. Tell him you are giving it to him in Christ's name."

"Oh, Dad," I protested, "I can't do anything like that."

My father's voice was firm. "Go and do as I tell you."

So, reluctant and resisting, I ran after the old man and said, "Excuse me, sir. I give you this money in the name of Christ."

He stared at the dollar bill, then looked at me in utter amazement. A wonderful smile came to his face, a smile so full of life and beauty that I forgot that he was dirty and unshaven. I forgot that he was ragged and old. With a gesture that was almost courtly, he took off his hat. Graciously he said, "And I thank you, young sir, in the name of Christ."

All my irritation, all my annoyance faded away. The street, the houses, everything around me suddenly seemed beautiful because I had been part of a miracle that I have seen many times since—the transformation that comes over people when you think of them as children of God, when you offer them love in the name of a baby born two thousand years ago in a stable in Bethlehem, a person who still lives and walks with us and makes his presence known.

That was my Christmas discovery that year—the gold of human dignity that lies hidden in every living soul, waiting to shine through if only we'll give it a chance.

II

The telephone call to my father came late at night, and from a most unlikely place—a house in the red-light district of the city. The woman who ran the house said that one of the girls who worked there was very ill, perhaps dying. The girl was calling for a minister. Somehow the woman had heard of my father. Would he come?

My father never failed to respond to such an appeal. Quietly he explained to my mother where he was going. Then his eyes fell upon me. "Get your coat, Norman," he said. "I want you to come too."

My mother was aghast. "You don't mean you'd take a fifteen-year-old boy into a place like that!"

My father said, "There's a lot of sin and sadness and despair in human life. Norman can't be shielded from it forever."

We walked through the snowy streets, and I remember how

the Christmas trees glowed and winked in the darkness. We came to the place, a big, old frame house. A woman opened the door and led us to an upstairs room. There, lying in a big brass bed, was a pathetic, doll-like young girl, so white and frail that she seemed like a child, scarcely older than I was.

Before he became a minister, my father had been a physician, and he knew the girl was gravely ill. When he sat on the edge of the bed, the girl reached for his hand. She whispered that she had come from a good Christian home and was sorry for the things she had done and the life she had led. She said she knew she was dying and that she was afraid. "I've been so bad," she said. "So bad."

I stood there listening. I didn't know what anybody could do to help her. But my father knew. He put both his big strong hands around her small one. He said, "There is no such thing as a bad girl. There are girls who act badly sometimes, but there are no bad girls—or bad boys either—because God made them and he makes all things good. Do you believe in Jesus?" The girl nodded. He continued, "Then let me hear you say, 'Dear Jesus, forgive me for my sins.'" She repeated those words. "Now," he said, "God loves you, his child who has strayed, and has forgiven you, and no matter when the time comes, he will take you to your heavenly home."

If I live to be a hundred, I will never forget the feeling of power and glory that came into that room as my father then prayed for that dying girl. There were tears on the faces of the other women standing there, and on my own too, because everything sordid, everything corrupt was simply swept away. There was beauty in that place of evil. The love born in Bethlehem was revealing itself again on a dark and dismal street in Cincinnati, Ohio, and nothing could withstand it. Nothing.

So that was the gift I received that Christmas, the frankincense—knowledge that there is good in all people, even the sad and the forlorn, and that no one need be lost because of past mistakes.

<hr>

III

<hr>

It was Christmas Eve in Brooklyn. I was feeling happy because things were going well with my church. As a young bachelor minister I had just had a fine visit with some parishioners and was saying goodbye to them on their porch.

All around us houses were decorated in honor of Christ's birthday. Suddenly a pair of wreaths on the house across the street caught my eye. One had the traditional red bow, bright and gay. But the ribbon on the other was a somber black—the symbol of a death in the family, a funeral wreath.

Something about that unexpected juxtaposition of joy and sorrow made a strange impression on me. I asked my host about it. He said that a young couple with small children lived in the house, but he did not know them. They were new in the neighborhood.

I said good night and walked down the street. But before I had gone far, something made me turn back. I did not know those people either. But it was Christmas Eve, and if there was joy or suffering to be shared, my calling was to share it.

Hesitantly I went up to the door and rang the bell. A tall young man opened the door. I told him that I was a minister whose church was in the neighborhood. I had seen the wreaths, I said, and wanted to offer my sympathy.

"Come in," he said quietly.

The house seemed very still. In the living room a coal fire was burning. In the center of the room was a small casket. In it was the body of a little girl about six years old. I can see her yet, lying there in a pretty, freshly ironed white dress. Nearby was an empty chair where the young man had been sitting, keeping watch beside the body of his child.

I was so moved that I could barely speak. *What a Christmas Eve,* I thought. Alone in a new neighborhood, no friends or relatives, a crushing loss. The young man seemed to read my thoughts. "It's all right," he said, as if he were reassuring me. "She's with the Lord, you know." His wife, he said, was upstairs with their two smaller children. He took me to meet her.

The young mother was reading to two small boys. She had a lovely face, sad yet serene. And suddenly I knew why this little family had been able to hang two wreaths on the door—one signifying life, the other, death. They had been able to do it because they knew it was all one process, all part of God's wonderful and merciful and perfect plan for all of us. They had heard the great promise that underlies Christmas: "Because I live, ye shall live also" (John 14:19). They had heard it and they believed it. That was why they could move forward together with love and dignity, courage and acceptance.

So that was the gift I received that year, the reaffirmation that the myrrh in the Christmas story is not just a reminder of death, but a symbol of the love that triumphs over death.

The young couple asked if they could join my church. They did, and we became good friends. Many years have passed since then, but not one has gone by without a Christmas card from some member of that family expressing love and gratitude.

But I am the one who is grateful.

Christmas—
As Mysterious as Ever

Doris Swehla

December 1986

*P*hyllis wasn't an easy child to love. I wanted the best for her and I prayed for God to bless her, but sometimes I did wish she wasn't in the particular Sunday school class I taught. Phyllis had stringy hair, dirty fingernails, and a runny nose. She kept apart from the rest of the children and she walked with a sort of stomp. Besides that, she never sat still, she hated to be touched, and she always had to have the last word.

I was twenty years old, and that year I supervised my first Christmas program at the big old stone church, Tabernacle Baptist, on Chicago's West Side. Early in Advent I held the typed pages of the Nativity script in my hand as I stood before the assembled children.

"If you'd like a speaking part in the program, raise your hand," I said, and almost every hand shot up. Not Phyllis's, of course. When everyone who wanted a part had one, I still had a few left.

"Phyllis," I said, "wouldn't you like just a few words to say in the program?"

"Who said I was coming to your program?" she asked, arms folded across her chest and chair tipped precariously on its back legs. "I'm probably going to a party that night," she said grandly.

Lord, I prayed silently, *please help me love Phyllis.*

"Well, I do have a few more parts if you change your mind."

"I won't," Phyllis said, and she didn't.

On the afternoon of the dress rehearsal, the children sat in the darkened front pews of the church whispering to each other as the adults put final touches on the bath-towel headdresses of the shepherds and the tinsel halos of the angels.

"Okay, take your places," I called from the back of the sanctuary.

The reader began: "In those days a decree went out . . ." A shiver rippled over me. Again I was immersed in the age-old story.

"Mary doesn't act like she's gonna have a baby," muttered a husky little voice behind me. Phyllis might not have any desire to be in the program, but she wouldn't miss the rehearsal!

"Shhhh!" I whispered, reaching back to pat Phyllis's hand.

She jerked it away, saying, "Okay! Okay!"

In the last scene, only a spotlight shone on the holy family, and the children hummed "Silent Night." It was beautiful—but who was that moving in front of the manger? Phyllis! You never knew where that child was going to pop up next. Now she stuck her hand into the manger, squeezed the doll's arm, and disappeared back into the shadows.

"Phyllis," I called, "what are you doing up there?"

"I'm just looking," she said. "Besides it's not a baby. It's just a doll. I felt it."

Lord, please help me love Phyllis.

"All right," I said to the cast. "Everyone be here at six-thirty so that you'll be in costume and ready to start promptly at seven. See you tonight."

Phyllis stomped up the aisle with the rest of the departing children. *With any luck at all,* I thought, *she will have had enough this afternoon and won't be back tonight.* I knew this wasn't a Christian reaction, but I did want the program to go smoothly.

By six-forty-five the air was bristling with excitement back-stage. Angels helped drape each other's bedsheet robes. Joseph and the Wise Men adjusted the beard wires that hooked over their ears. Mary stared into the mirror trying to capture just the right look for the mother of the Savior. I moved from group to group, helping where I could. There was no Phyllis to be seen and I began to relax.

Just a minute before seven, Mrs. Wright entered. In her arms she held her tiny new baby. All wrapped in white, he would replace the doll we'd used in rehearsals. "He's just been fed," she said, "so he should sleep during the program."

"You can put him in the manger just as the lights go down," I whispered.

As the organ chimed indicating the beginning of the service, I took my prompter's seat in the front pew. With the opening strains of "Watchman, Tell Us of the Night," the lights came up on the manger scene, and the narrator began.

But instead of the familiar shiver as I heard the beginning of the Christmas Scripture, I felt something bump my knee and give a little shove. "Move over," muttered an all-too-familiar voice. "I decided not to go to the party."

Not taking my eyes from the drama unfolding up front, I moved over and reached out to pat Phyllis's knee. She flung my hand back into my lap.

I'm trying, Lord, I thought.

The angels sang to the shepherds. The shepherds went to Bethlehem and took a lamb for the baby. The Wise Men went to see Herod and then to the stable. And Mary sat there "pondering these things in her heart." It was lovely. Phyllis sat beside me so quietly that I forgot all about her, and when I realized she was gone, it was too late.

She stomped her way right up to the manger, just as she had done during the rehearsal. But this time she stiffened, awestruck, then turned, eyes wide with wonder, and came hurrying back to me.

"He's alive!" she said to me in a penetrating whisper.

Across the aisle, someone asked, "What did she say?"

"She said, 'He's alive!'"

Like ripples in a pond, the word passed from pew to pew, all the way to the back of the sanctuary. "He's alive . . . alive . . . alive." The air grew electric as one by one the people in the congregation felt the living presence of the baby in Bethlehem.

Here was the real reason we all were celebrating. *He's alive! Emmanuel—God with us, God incarnate.* A tough, unruly little girl had brought the majestic Christmas message home. *God is alive!*

The lights came up, and when we stood to sing "Joy to the

World! the Lord Is Come," the sound rocked our big old church as never before.

I put my arm around Phyllis's tight little shoulders. "You were the best part of the program," I said into her ear, drawing her close to my side.

"I wasn't in your program," she said. But she didn't push me away.

His
Mysterious
Ways

A FEW DAYS BEFORE Christmas 2000, I dropped off a roll of film from a recent trip I'd taken with my friend Jack to see the fall colors in eastern Tennessee. I had an hour before the pictures were ready. As I did some last-minute shopping, I thought about seeing everyone at our family's annual holiday get-together. I was looking forward to it, but I couldn't help feeling that Christmas hadn't been the same since my grandmother passed away in 1995.

The whole family used to gather at Nana's little farmhouse in Maynardville, Tennessee. There were so many of us that we had to eat in shifts. But somehow we all managed to crowd into Nana's living room to open our presents around the tree. Nana would sit in her rocking chair, smiling when she saw how excited we grandkids were. My uncles capped off the night with a big fireworks display that had us oohing and aahing all the way home.

If only I could just see one more wonderful Christmas at Nana's house, I thought wistfully.

I finished my shopping and picked up my photos. On the way to the car, I opened the package. I couldn't believe my eyes. Superimposed over the autumn foliage in the first shot was an image of Nana sitting in her rocking chair holding a Christmas present. I flipped through the rest of the photos—double exposures, all of them, showing my family celebrating Christmas at Nana's house. How had they turned up on that roll of film?

As soon as I got home I called Jack. "I loaded that roll into your camera," he said. "I found it on the floor of your car, and I just figured you'd dropped it. When did you say those pictures are from?"

I looked more closely at the photographs. There was Nana. And Granddaddy, who'd passed away more than ten years ago. "It looks like they're from Christmas 1989," I said.

Jack whistled. "That certainly was an old roll of film."

"But, Jack, where did it come from? I've only had that car for two years."

—Teresa Atkins, *December 2002*

The Man Who Wanted to Go Home

JIMMY GUPTON

December 1989

Another Christmas coming . . . toy commercials and holiday specials on television. And here I was, an old man spending another evening in front of the tube.

Why, Lord? I asked him for the thousandth time. *Why won't you just go ahead and take me home?*

I'd been a Christian all my life and figured the Almighty didn't mind my taking a familiar tone with him. *Ninety-three years is long enough on this earth, I've lived a full life, and I can't see where I'm much good to you or anyone else anymore.*

When my wife was alive it was different. But Bess had been gone for seven years now, and lately it was getting harder to go through the motions. Christmas, for example—I hadn't even bothered to get the big silver tree out of the box in the attic this year. It was a pretty thing, but attaching 150 branches was a big job. After my eyes went bad, I'd had to take an ice pick to feel for the holes. With only me here, why bother?

A rock group came on the screen to sing "Jingle Bells." *You see, Lord, I'm not going to be able to take care of this place much longer, and you know I don't want to go somewhere else.* My two sons and their families kept asking me to move in with one of them, but I'm a stubborn kind of fellow. I liked it here, liked my independence.

This past year, though . . . It was a small house, but it was getting to be too much. The roof was leaking, the wallpaper peeling. *Why can't I just come home, Lord, and not fool with an interim move?*

On the screen now were pictures of the Salvation Army shelter in downtown Charlotte, part of a series on homelessness at Christmas. "There are over two hundred women sleeping here tonight," an announcer said, "out of work and out of hope." I sure felt sorry for those people. But I hardly had enough money to cover my own expenses, much less make a donation. At about ten o'clock I switched off the set, turned off the lights, and said my usual prayers before climbing into bed.

Instead of falling asleep, though, I kept seeing those women at the shelter. I'd always given to the poor when I was able. Surely it was someone else's turn now. But that news report wouldn't leave me alone. There were those women needing help. *Just like me*, I thought.

I sat up in bed. *What if two needy folks were to put their needs together? What if one of these women were to move in here, take care of the house in exchange for a place to live?*

The next morning I telephoned the shelter. "If you're serious, Mr. Gupton," the manager said, "I'll ask around."

A few days after Christmas he called back: "Would you consider taking in a married couple?"

"Well, now . . ." I hadn't counted on two people. "It's such a small house," I apologized. "The spare room's barely big enough for one."

"What I was thinking," the man went on, "was that the wife could keep house and the husband could look after the yard. As for the size of the room, I'm sure anything with a door on it would look like a palace to them right now."

The manager paused a moment to let this sink in. "I think I've got the perfect couple. Tony and Pam Davis."

Both Davises had lost their jobs. Unable to meet rent payments, they'd been evicted from their home, and ended up sleeping at the shelter at night and job hunting during the day. "It's hard to impress an employer wearing wrinkled clothing, having no permanent address."

"Send them on over," I said. "We'll give it a try."

It looked as though it was going to work. Pam was a little shy at first, but before the week was out we were chatting like old friends. She told me she'd been a waitress while Tony worked as a carpet installer, until both places of employment went out of business the same month. With downcast eyes she described what it had been like to be in a Salvation Army shelter at Christmastime.

It was nice to have someone keeping house, cooking meals, taking care of the yard again. Wonderful to have them care enough to escort me to the senior citizens' center, to drive me to church.

About three months after they'd come, though, Pam said she

needed to talk to me. The two of us had just finished lunch; Tony had found a job with another carpet installation company and was gone during the day.

"I don't know how to say this, Mr. Gupton," she began.

Oh, no! I thought. *She's going to tell me they're moving out now that Tony's working.*

Pam got up and started piling dishes in the sink. "I know I should have told you in the beginning," she said, "but I was afraid you wouldn't let us stay—and you might want us to leave after you hear this. But I can't put off telling you any longer. . . ."

She twisted the dishrag in her hands. "You see, I . . . I'm . . ." She lifted her dark eyes to stare into mine. "I'm going to have a baby."

So that was it! "Well, you're right about one thing," I said. "I hadn't counted on three of you, that's for sure." She turned away, looking down at the sink. "But I certainly can't let you go back on the streets," I assured her. "Not with a baby coming." I tried to keep my voice calm, but my mind was shouting, *A baby! Where will we put a baby?*

"I know there's not much room here," Pam said as if reading my thoughts. "But if we move the dresser out of our room, I'm sure we could squeeze a small crib in, and I'll try to keep the baby quiet so it won't disturb you too much."

The months flew by. Pam shifted the tiny room around to sandwich a crib between the bed and the wall, bought diapers and bottles, and began a whirlwind of painting and wallpapering all over the house.

And before I knew it, a redheaded baby girl named Sabrina

arrived. Pam tried to keep her quiet and out of my way as much as possible. Soon she was three months old, then five months old, and then it was the middle of December—almost Christmas again.

I was sitting in the living room one evening reading the second chapter of Luke as I always did at this time of year: "And she brought forth her firstborn son," I read, "and laid him in a manger; because there was no room for them in the inn" (verse 7).

That must have saddened God, I thought, feeling pretty good that I'd found room for the Davis family, though in some ways it had been an inconvenience. Even as I thought about the crowded inn, though, I knew that wasn't the point of the story. What God had wanted, far more than a room at the inn, was for people to open their hearts and make room for his Son.

Perhaps that's what he'd been trying to get me to do. Sure, I'd made room for the Davises in my house, but maybe God had been trying to get me to make room in my heart.

The winter wind was beating at the old windows, seeping round the newspapers Pam had stuffed into the cracks. I got up and stoked the fire in the wood stove—we had to keep the place warm for the baby. *You know*, I told myself, *if we slid the couch back against the wall, I believe there'd be room for a playpen in here. Can't keep a growing child cooped up in a bedroom.*

I walked over to the stairs. "Tony! Pam!" I called.

"What is it, Mr. Gupton?" Tony asked, hurrying down.

"Is something wrong?" said Pam, following behind him, alarm in her eyes.

"You bet something's wrong," I said. "Here it is, almost Christmas, and we don't have a tree up!"

"We thought about that," Tony admitted. "But trees are so expensive."

"That's so," I agreed. "But I happen to know where there's a beautiful tree just waiting to be put up. It's in a box in the attic now, but when it's standing tall and grand with the colored lights beaming across its silver branches, you never saw anything so pretty in all your life. With a child in the house, we've got to have a Christmas tree!"

Tony and Pam raced up the rickety stairs to the attic and dragged down the bulky box. Pam unpacked the branches; I fluffed out the tinsel "needles" and passed them to Tony to insert in the holes. It was fun doing it together. I coached Tony as he set the tree in the revolving stand I'd made out of an old TV antenna many years before. Then I switched on the multicolored flood-light and sat back to enjoy their oohs and aahs as the tree started to turn like a silver ballerina.

About that time, we heard a hungry wail from upstairs. Pam ran up and brought Sabrina down. She looked surprised, but pleased, when I motioned for her to hand the baby to me while she went off to the kitchen to heat a bottle. Sabrina and I sat there, eyeing each other silently. I felt kind of awkward. After all, it had been some time since I'd conversed with a young child.

Sabrina studied my face intently, and for a moment I thought she was going to cry. But instead she broke into a laugh and reached a chubby little hand toward my cheek. I laughed too when I realized she was trying to catch the fleeting reflections from the tree. The touch of her hand made me think of another child, born on Christmas so many years ago.

I looked at Tony, arranging candles in the window, listened to Pam humming a carol out in the kitchen. And I whispered a prayer to the one who has our times in his keeping.

"Thank you, Lord, for letting me see another Christmas . . . for leaving me here though I fussed and fretted. Sometimes it takes a baby to remind an old man what your world is all about."

Blessed Are Those
in the Lobby

RICHARD CRENNA

December 1993

When I was growing up, a typical Christmas morning was spent quietly having breakfast with my parents in a local restaurant. Resting on the table would be the gift my folks had just presented to me after the waitress took our order. Of course I was happy, but it wasn't like racing downstairs in your own house in the morning to find a present under the tree.

We always ate out because we lived in the Stephens, a hotel in downtown Los Angeles. The seventy-two-room residential hotel was owned by my parents. It was during the Depression, and Mother managed the hotel to supplement Dad's income as a pharmacist. Growing up in the city had its benefits. I loved riding streetcars; took my first communion at the nearby church, Precious Blood; and attended a local school with Asian, Latino, and African-American kids. Though I was a minority, we kids were never aware of differences; we were friends. All in all, I considered myself privileged.

But Christmas in a hotel always had a downside for me. I never had a real family Christmas. Friends told me of houses fragrant with roasting turkey, and of relatives gathering around the tree in the living room. Since Mom, Dad, and I lived in only two rooms, our tree always went up in the hotel lobby. So I never had anything to brag about. With me it was always, "Here comes Christmas again, and I've got to go down and wish a happy holiday to all those sad-eyed people in the lobby." For the Stephens was full of unfortunates who spent Christmas alone.

Some were characters straight from Damon Runyon stories—gamblers, con men, bookies, and former jockeys. Others were right out of *Ripley's Believe It or Not!* Like the "Most Tattooed Man," who was our night clerk—his real name was Ted Rockwell, and his body was covered with tattoos of his name, in every language, as well as in Chinese pictographs, Morse code, and signal flags.

Then there was the "World's Greatest Thief," who, it was said, had walked out the front door of Abercrombie & Fitch in New York City with a canoe and then went back the next day for the paddles. An elderly, silver-haired man, he had already paid his debt to society.

Our femme fatale, Mac Taylor, who had lived at the Stephens for more than twenty years, fancied herself a movie star. Then there was "Tumbleweed," who looked just like his name when he came down the street after a night out. He bounced from side to side off of buildings before rolling his way into the hotel. One night while we were all sitting around the big Atwater Kent radio in the lobby, somebody dropped him inside the door, saying, "I think this belongs to you."

Mom helped him up to his room and tucked him into bed. She was a mother figure to all our seventy-two guests, though she made sure none of the bookies or gamblers plied their trade in the hotel. The only time I saw her angry was the night a lady checked in and within fifteen minutes had hung a red light bulb over her transom. Mother put her out immediately.

In my young mind I disdained these people as has-beens and losers. And I often took advantage of their foibles. The "Germ Man" had a phobia about bacteria and always wore a face mask. When meeting him on the stairs, I'd take great delight in sneezing as loudly as I could and as many times as possible. He'd bolt madly for his room and Mother would scold me for my unkind behavior.

Watching this strange assortment of people, I believe, actually started me on my acting career. I used to mimic the things they did, especially the drunks. At an early age I could fall down a flight of stairs without hurting myself. I must have rolled into the lobby of the Stephens a thousand times.

It was only natural for me to take drama at Virgil Junior High. The CBS and NBC radio studios were nearby, and a friend and I fished through their garbage bins for discarded scripts. We used them to stage our own plays, adding some imaginative sound effects.

One day, while we were playing football on the playground, our drama teacher came out and said, "Boys, they're auditioning for a new radio program at station KFI. I want you all to try out. It will be good experience."

Dirty and sweaty, we traipsed over to KFI to audition for a program called *Boy Scout Jamboree*. It was a comedy about a troop of nine Scouts who did everything wrong. A group of us were hired for twenty-five cents per Saturday show, and I ended up staying on the program for many years. I played Herman, a prototype of all the other goofy, adenoidal, adolescent kids I later portrayed on *The Great Gildersleeve*, *The Hardy Family*, and *One Man's Family*.

This led to my being considered for the role of Henry Aldrich on *The Aldrich Family* radio series. Another actor, Dickie Jones, and I were asked to go to New York City to audition in January 1942. As a sixteen-year-old, I was thrilled to be going all the way across the country, even though I knew only one of us would get the part.

But I wasn't expecting what happened that Christmas Eve. Mother and Dad ushered me into the pine-scented lobby, where I saw all the residents gathered around the tree. The hand-cranked Victrola was screeching out Christmas carols.

It was a surprise Christmas celebration and going-away party for me. I was stunned. Each resident had a gift for me. I had no idea that they really cared. Mae Taylor presented me with monogrammed handkerchiefs in a fancy box. Tumbleweed, sober for a change, handed me a pocketknife with all kinds of built-in tools. The World's Greatest Thief, his sky-blue eyes shining, gestured to the floor. There sat an expensive set of matched Hartmann leather luggage.

"When you go to New York, Dick," he said, "you've got to look successful." I glanced at Mom apprehensively. But she smiled and pointed to the zippered canvas covers with my name stitched on them. The World's Greatest Thief had purchased this luggage—for me.

Even the Germ Man and the drunks I had relentlessly mimicked offered me their congratulations. I remembered my old priest saying that if you "bless them that curse you . . . ye shall be the children of the Highest" (Luke 6:28, 35). I hadn't actually cursed any of these people, but I certainly had made fun of them. And now they were paying me back with kindness and encouragement. Sad-eyed people in the lobby? Well, here I was, misty-eyed at their loving support. It was now clear: The men and women I had once written off as has-beens and weirdos were instead children of the Highest.

For the first time, I began to see that people are equal. And I understood Mother's compassion for former thieves, gamblers, and bookies: You love people for what they are, not for what you wish them to be.

Soon I was on the train toward New York with my father, who had taken time off to chaperon me. A fellow passenger finished exclaiming about his own holiday, then he turned to me. "And how about you?" he asked.

I leaned back and smiled. "It was my best Christmas ever," I said. "I spent it with . . . my family."

Christmas in Dixie

LYDA JEAN BENNETT

December 1995

When my husband, Earl, and I were kids, neither of our families was able to give us much of a Christmas. I guess that's why we've always made such a big thing of it for our kids. Eleven years ago my mother brought us an outdoor set of Nativity figures that light up, and Earl built a plank stable to house them. At that time our six children and seventeen grandchildren were living either in our country farmhouse or in trailers scattered throughout our eight-acre hilltop property. A few days before Christmas, my brother Bill helped us build a big bonfire in front of the setup. Earl plucked "Jingle Bells" on the banjo, the boys joined in on guitars, and we raised a joyful noise. That year it was just family.

The next year we put up more lights, and people started stopping their cars and rolling down their windows and listening to the music. Our family was so big, a few more never hurt, so we started inviting people up.

Finally I said to Earl, "Well, if people want to come, who's it going to bother? We're stuck out here in the boonies." We decided to do it right, because I know too well there are people who don't have much Christmas.

Everybody in the family with a paycheck started putting aside twenty-five dollars a week. We didn't have much of a system—just made things up as we went along. It was all handmade, homemade, folksy Christmas stuff, but people seemed to like it. Soon hundreds were coming from all over the South, so we built a barnlike building to accommodate them. By the time we got it finished, it was bigger than our house, with public restrooms, and chairs for the elderly.

One night during our fifth year, I found a seventeen-year-old girl in a raggedy jacket staring at the Nativity scene. She looked at me and asked, "Lady, do you mind telling me what this is all about?"

My jaw dropped. "Do you mean to tell me that you don't know the story of Christmas?"

She shook her head. "No, ma'am, I reckon I don't."

I told her the best I could about the birth of Jesus. When I was done, she nodded her head like she was thinking real hard and thanked me to death. I walked home with tears in my eyes and vowed that we would tell the Christmas story in some way on our hill for people like that girl.

We came up with the idea of soft-sculpture dolls, as big as a person and with nylon faces and hands. We made patterns and sewed clothes. All the next year we gathered material, cut out pieces, and stuffed bodies. We made different scenes and lettered

Scripture verses on plywood signs. In the first scene we suspended an angel from a tree and had him telling Mary that she was going to be the mother of Jesus.

In the next scene we put pregnant Mary on an oak-log donkey going to Bethlehem. My daughter Judy painted a somber face on this Mary. The third scene was the shepherds, and we made stuffed woolly lambs. I guess they looked lifelike, because an old dog carried one off. The next one was the Nativity scene with the Baby Jesus in the manger. That baby doll was special because my granddaughter's daddy gave it to her.

We had Wise Men on plywood camels heading toward King Herod, and our last scene was the flight into Egypt. This Mary too has a particular look on her face, like she's thinking hard and is scared about how she's going to take care of her baby. I was most proud of that work.

Every year after that we told more stories with soft-sculpture figures—the Christmas guest, the lamplighter, an old hay wagon full of folks going home for Christmas, a military camp scene to honor the troops overseas in Desert Storm.

In our tenth year, 1993, we figured we had about fifty thousand visitors. The state mental hospital got special permission for a night trip. The patients were so excited that they gasped when they saw those seventy-five thousand lights. That year folks roasted nineteen thousand hot dogs over the wood fire, and I served 2718 gallons of hot chocolate. But it was also the year that something spooky started happening. Lights started going out. Some days we had to put in a hundred new ones.

We were expecting our biggest year ever in 1994 because we

had been listed in a travel book. We added fifty thousand lights. We worked all August and September unrolling strings of lights and checking them, working eight hours a day. We opened to the public on Thanksgiving.

That night somebody came through and pulled the lights off fifty trees. Down by the road a string of one hundred lights ended up with just eight left. Somebody stole Scrooge. Vandals pried open the gingerbread house and stole things. We tried to keep it quiet because we figured we didn't want to be putting ideas into kids' heads.

The big trouble started on Wednesday, December 7. We caught seven teenage boys trying to knock over the life-size ply-wood horse figures hitched to the hay wagon. Earl finally got the teenagers off the property with the help of some visitors, but they cussed and fought him all the way.

We got to bed at one-thirty A.M. on Sunday, December 11. Two hours later I woke up to a thump, thump, thump. I told Earl, "They're tearing the wagon up!" He jumped out of bed and crashed out the back door with me right behind him. The vandals dashed to their cars and took off.

We stood out there in the dark shivering. Things got real quiet. I saw Frosty the Snowman all beat up, and I thought, *Oh, dear Lord.* If a tornado had come through, I don't think it could have been any worse. My soft-sculpture dolls were hanging in trees, and decorations had been thrown into mudholes along the side of the road. They were scattered for about four or five miles. Judy told me, "Mama, you don't want to go any further. They've torn up your Nativity scene."

As we stood waiting for the sheriff that morning, I could see how bad it all was. Every figure had its head cut off, clothes ripped away, and body mutilated. They had cut the stuffed animals and had torn the head off Baby Jesus and thrown him in the mud.

When I looked down that hill, seeing nothing but destruction after we had worked so hard, it was as if a family member had died. My insides collapsed and my heart could hardly beat. We had spent all our time and money, and we had never asked for anything in return except for people to enjoy themselves. The blood was pulsating in my head. I wondered how the world had come to the awful point where, just for meanness, people would sneak on our place and tear up everything that we had done to make a nice Christmas for the community.

I was still dizzy when a woman who said she was from Alabama tried to console me between her sobs. Right behind her came a woman who told me she had driven about sixty miles from Augusta with her granddaughter. Then came a hard-nosed bachelor we knew from town. The little girl looked up at him and asked, "Mister, why did they do this?"

I just stood there, numb. I needed to know what right anybody had to hurt a little girl who just wanted to see Rudolph.

Next thing I knew, that hard-nosed bachelor was crying too. He fished into his pocket and pulled out a one-hundred-dollar bill, which he handed to me. "Here's your first donation to repair it," he said huskily.

Then a neighbor drove up with his pickup loaded with decorations he had gathered from the roadside. A lawyer friend came by and started a repair fund. But soon the day was gone, and we had hardly begun to fix things. We were all feeling mighty awful, but I said, "Well, the lights are still pretty. We've got the building and the hot dogs, and people don't know about this, so if they come, we owe it to them to open."

So we did. I worked inside, keeping the hot chocolate flowing. Around closing time Bill came in and said, "You won't believe this, but somebody set up the displays down the hill."

"Who?" I asked.

"The people. They went into the mudholes and ditches and brought things back. They set the wagon up; the figures are sitting on it. Anything that was out of its display box, they've put back the best they could."

At eleven o'clock that night, Judy called after she had walked back to her trailer. "Mama, your Nativity scene's back up. You won't believe what people have done."

By Monday morning a radio station had started collecting donations. Firefighters from nearby Richmond County organized volunteers and donations of decorations. But the thing that touched me the most was the phone calls. As soon as I hung up, the phone rang again. A pilot said, "Mrs. Bennett, I've never been to your place, but when I fly over it, that's the warmest feeling in the world, and I know I'm home safe once again."

A lady said, "If you don't fix anything else, make sure the soldier scene goes back up. My son was in Desert Storm, and he had never seen his baby. We took pictures of the baby at the military camp display and sent them to him, and that was the first look he got at his baby."

A woman from South Carolina called. "My husband and I had been coming every year. Last year we were going to get a divorce. It was a sad Christmas, but I decided I would take my little girl over to you anyway. When we arrived, lo and behold, there was my husband. We decided to make another go of it, and now we're happier than we've ever been."

I must have had a hundred callers that Monday, each one with a tale to tell of how much Christmas in Dixie had meant to them. That night I thought, *Well, Sunday was the worst day of my life, and now today has been the best.*

On Tuesday, with the help of the firefighters and all the volunteers we could use, we glued, patched, wired, and sewed everything back together. It wasn't one hundred percent, but it was good enough. As I sewed the head back on Baby Jesus and put him in the manger, I remembered something that had happened the first year we had done the manger scene. A blind lady in her eighties named Alice was brought over one evening. I took her hand, read her the Scriptures on the board and then described each scene. When we got to the manger, she let go of my hand and went in, hugged the figures and called out in prayer, "Oh, Lord! Oh, Jesus!"

Some fifty people watched her reverently. I thought, *Those figures are only fabric, stuffing, and paint—just material things. But don't tell Alice that. Because right now she's hugging Baby Jesus.*

Now, as I laid him back in the manger, I figured the vandals had miscalculated. They too thought what we had was just boards and lights and material. But I learned that it was more. It was a place where families came back together, where the lonely found a spot by the fire, where people from institutions felt normal, where a rich lady in a fur coat could stand next to a dirty, runny-nosed little boy roasting a hot dog.

This was where the story of Baby Jesus could make Christmas real again, where spiritual awakenings could take place. I've got to tell you, I know. Because my own tired and torn-up spirits had been warmed up pretty good. And it was Christmas in Dixie again.

A Blue Christmas?

December 1999

*L*ectures. Term papers. Finals. Grades. College was nothing but pressure on top of pressure. I was carrying a full course load at Bauder in Arlington, Texas, the fall semester of my sophomore year and feeling like I had a weight the size of the Lone Star State on my shoulders. The fact that it was Friday didn't matter one bit. I was looking at a weekend of studying. I wondered where I would find time even for church on Sunday.

I drove my usual route home to my parents' and hoped the familiar sights along the way would ease my stress. But the big old weeping willow I'd watched grow from a skinny sapling, my high school, the garland-wrapped streetlights downtown—that day they didn't do a thing for me.

I turned onto North Center Street and drove by the lawn with the big plastic Nativity figures. The crib was empty, and the light in the cow had burned out. I slowed the car while some tall boys moved their football game out of the street. Up ahead was the weather-beaten two-story house that always stuck in my mind. The paint was chipped and peeling, the steps to the front porch sagged, and I imagined big empty rooms inside. The frail old man who lived there was sitting out front, as usual, his black Lab lying lazily in the tall grass at his feet. *He's got his Bible out again*, I noted. Once I'd heard him reciting passages to the dog! A couple times I'd felt the urge to stop and say hi, just talk to him for a few minutes, see if he was all right, but I was always too busy. I glanced in my rearview mirror. "Reading the Bible to a dog," I murmured, hitting the brakes. "How lonely can a person get?"

In the next open driveway I turned the car around, breaking up the boys' ball game again. I parked in front of the run-down house and got out of my car. "Hi," I called to the old man, suddenly feeling awkward. "Nice day, isn't it?"

"Come on and sit awhile," he said, scooting over on the steps to make room for me. "I'm Diggs," he said, "and that's my dog, Blue."

"Pleasure to meet you, Mr. Diggs. Everybody calls me Misty." We shook hands, and I took a seat. Up close the man didn't seem so frail. His eyes were soft and content. "I've often seen you out here reading," I said, reaching to pat Blue's head.

Mr. Diggs smiled. "Mostly I read the Bible. I have plenty of time for reading these days."

"You live alone?" I asked.

"I wouldn't put it that way exactly," Mr. Diggs said. "My wife and most of my friends are gone from this world, but I'm never alone. Not as long as I have my faith." Blue let loose an expressive whine and nosed Mr. Diggs's shoe. "Yes, yes, boy," he laughed, "and I've got you too. But that goes without saying." He leaned over to rub Blue's back, and I saw how much he loved him.

"Blue likes to listen to me read," Mr. Diggs said. "You have time for a story, Misty?"

"Maybe just one," I said, getting a little nervous about everything I had to do.

The old man turned to the story of the first Christmas in Luke. *I hope this doesn't take too long*, I thought. Blue rested his chin on his crossed paws as if pleased to sit and listen all day. I scratched my knee and tried to sneak a peek at my watch.

"'Behold,'" Mr. Diggs read, slowing down as he repeated the angel's holy announcement, "'I bring you good tidings of great joy . . .'"

Christmas had always been a joyful time for me too, but that year it had taken a back seat to school. Everything had. I stayed quiet, though, till Mr. Diggs finished. When he had, part of me was sorry. He had a way about him that was calming, and while he was reading, his voice a little like a good preacher's, I'd almost forgotten my worries. "I'd better get going," I said. "My parents will be holding dinner, and I have loads of schoolwork."

Mr. Diggs invited me back anytime. "Old Blue and I will be here. You can count on that."

I said I'd stop by again, but pretty quickly I fell back into my routine of studying, studying, and more studying, and worrying about studying in between. On the day before school let out for Christmas break, I drove down North Center Street again. Mr. Diggs was there on the porch, his head in his hands. Something was wrong. I stretched my neck to look into the tall grass. Blue! He was gone! *No way could I stop. What would I say?* I sped by. At home I threw myself onto my bed, feeling guilty.

When I refused my mom's meatloaf and mashed potatoes, she figured I had a flu bug. I knew different. I was sick of myself. It was time to get my nose out of my books and do something that wasn't about me.

On Christmas Eve I drove the familiar route toward school. I didn't have class; Mom had said I could invite Mr. Diggs over for Christmas dinner. I turned down North Center Street, passed the big Nativity scene and parked in front of the old house. *Why isn't he outside on a nice day like this?* I wondered, walking up to the porch. I knocked hard on the door and heard shuffling footsteps inside. Mr. Diggs pulled open the door and smiled. "Come on in, Misty," he said. "What a surprise."

I stepped inside, and when he closed the door the house fell quiet. Blue was nowhere to be seen, except in pictures scattered all around the den. There were other pictures too, of Mr. Diggs and his wife, waving from a ship, sharing a beach umbrella, sitting at a tiny table in a fancy restaurant. But mostly there were pictures of Blue. Mr. Diggs saw me staring at the one of Blue swimming with a big stick in his mouth. "He played fetch in the gulf for two solid hours that day," he remembered. "There was a bit of an undertow, but Blue was a mighty strong swimmer."

Was? I looked at Mr. Diggs.

"Blue's disappeared," he said, his voice shaky. "I can't hardly sit out on the porch these days. It makes me miss him all the more."

"I'm sorry, Mr. Diggs. Really I am. Your wife, your friends . . . now Blue." I began to cry. He'd lost everything.

Mr. Diggs handed me his hankie. "Don't forget, Misty, I've got my faith. That's the constant in my life. Hard as they may be, the rough patches pass. I've prayed for Blue to come home, and now it's up to the Lord."

I sniffled. "But what if Blue doesn't come back . . . ever?"

"He's in the Lord's capable hands. So am I. So are you too, Misty."

I was amazed that even now he was ready to accept whatever God had in store.

"Do you believe in Christmas?" Mr. Diggs asked. "In the promise of Jesus' birth? God never leaves us. No matter what else may be happening in our lives, happy or sad, Christmas is coming. And Christmas always comes, Misty. You can count on that."

I dried my eyes. "That's why I stopped by, actually—to invite you to spend tomorrow with my family." Mr. Diggs accepted, and I raced home to tell Mom to set the extra place at our table.

When I arrived on Christmas Day to pick him up, Mr. Diggs was wearing an old gray suit and a tad too much aftershave. He offered his arm and escorted me to my car. As he held open my door, I noticed something in the distance: a parade of children coming up the street. I recognized the tall boys whose football game I'd disrupted. Younger kids led the pack. A black spot next to one of the kids started to take shape as they moved toward us. *Could it be?*

"Blue!" Mr. Diggs shouted, and his friend came running. The kids caught up and gathered around us, telling how they'd seen the dog several blocks away and knew he belonged on North Center Street. We all petted Blue and welcomed him home. "How 'bout taking a nap till I get back?" Mr. Diggs said. Blue circled a few times, then lay down in his spot in the tall grass. The neighborhood kids promised to keep an eye on him while they played outside with their new bikes and roller skates.

Mr. Diggs waved to them as we drove down North Center Street past the lawn with the big Nativity. The baby lay in the manger, and the light in the cow had been replaced. "See what I told you, Misty?" Mr. Diggs said. "Christmas always comes."

We enjoyed our day together, and when I brought Mr. Diggs home, Blue was there waiting.

Driving to school the first day classes resumed, I saw the old man at his usual post. This time, though, Blue wasn't the sole audience for his Bible reading. At Mr. Diggs's feet were nine or ten kids from the neighborhood. I honked and waved. College wasn't going to get any easier, but the rough patches would pass. And after all, Christmas was only a few hundred days away.

Traditions of Love

Keeping Christmas

DOROTHY WALWORTH

December 1947

*S*ome morning this December I will read an advertisement offering for sale, "Christmas novelties." It will leave me cold. An article on the woman's page will doubtless exhort me, "Aren't you tired of wrapping your packages in the same old red and green? Try yellow, for a change." But I *like* the same old red and green.

An up-to-date Santa Claus in a motorized sleigh is, to me, a monstrosity. I do not wish to hear new, strange Christmas music, though it may have the best of contemporary intentions. The old carols are the only music that warms my heart in the December cold. I hope no one will send me a Christmas card with modern-looking angels. Nor do I wish to hear the Christmas story except according to the Gospel of Saint Luke. Any other version, however brilliant, seems secondhand. But when I hear the words, "And there were in the same country shepherds abiding in the field, keeping watch over their flock by night," I become, once again, a humble, wondering child. I catch an authentic glimpse of the kingdom of heaven.

When this December comes, I know what I will be doing. It is what I have always done. My family will give me lists of what they want for Christmas. I will give them a list too—I can never think of anything I want in December, although I can think of plenty all the other months of the year. I will also mark down some names of people who don't expect presents, because remembering folks like that give us all a sort of blissful, floating feeling. I will not let myself be depressed when somebody says to me, "Christmas has become commercialized." Nonsense. Christmas is only commercialized for those who let it be that way. Nor will I agree when I hear that feeble, weary bromide, "Christmas is only for children." Nonsense again. The more we live, the more Christmas means. Christmas, though forever young, grows old along with us.

I will resolve to economize but, as usual, will be a bit extravagant. I will try to shop early but will be envious of those calm women who announce they have done everything by the middle of November. My husband and I will buy wreaths for the front windows of our house. So far we have never been able to afford wreaths for the sides and back. We will go out together and choose our Christmas tree. And just any old tree won't do! We always have our hearts set on a bushy tree that is too tall for our living room and has to be sawed off at the top.

Of course, I will get tired. I will have my secret disappointments too, because of those wishes on Christmas lists which I cannot fulfill. Probably I will get a cold. Somewhere in the midst of the rush, I will say to myself, "I just can't seem to feel the Christmas spirit yet this year." And I will get worried chills down my spine for fear that the day might come, and, in my hurry and fatigue, I might not feel the spirit.

However, just as I worry, the ancient bliss will begin to come over me. Little by little I will see our ordinary grocery store transformed by festoons of ground pine. All of Main Street will become rapturously different. My husband will call to me, "There's a carol on the radio," and we will listen. Both of us believe there are not enough carols on the radio throughout the Christmas season, and too many crowded at the end, into a few hours.

When the day approaches so near we can say, "next week," suddenly, I will not be at all tired. Who could be tired in the midst of a miracle? I will scan my lists again, feeling I have not given anyone half enough, and make a final, frenzied visit to the stores. My husband will be told not to look in the guest-room closet, and he will warn me not to look under the bed. Our house will fill with tissue paper. I am not good at doing up packages; I tie clumsy bows. But who cares? We all hope there will be snow for Christmas, but it really does not matter. As the miracle draws closer, everything else seems small. Nothing can harm the joy of Christmas, when I remember that the angel of the Lord's first words to the shepherds were: "Fear not: for, behold, I bring you good tidings."

The Christmas cards will begin to arrive, the cherished record of our friendships. Down from the attic will come our Christmas trimmings, which are, in their own way, the story of our married life. They have lasted a long time, because we have been so careful with them. Some ornaments we have had ever since we were married, like the star for the top of the tree. There are the red globes our daughter liked best when she was small, and the horn the kitten almost broke, which was saved in the nick of time. We will set on a table our simple crèche, with the figures of the holy family, along with an ox and an ass and the shepherds. We are always sure, each year, that the holy child has gotten lost somewhere among all the trimmings, but he is never lost. He lies, as always, in the manger, with the tiny gold light about his head.

On Christmas Eve my husband always has a hard time getting the tree into its metal stand. He pounds and thumps, while I hold on to the trunk. Finally it stands straight. Then we trim the tree with the lights, the ornaments, and, finally, the tinsel. Somehow, in the light from the tree, my husband always looks as young as the day we married, and he says I do too. On Christmas Eve, although we may be doing very ordinary things, I will feel the same almost unbearable excitement as I did when I was a child. Because something wonderful is about to happen. I will not be able to help thinking that, at that very moment, the Wise Men are seeing the star, and there is still no room at the inn.

When the tree is all decorated, I will sit down at the piano and my husband and I will sing the carols. We do not sound as fine as the radio, but we like it better. Of course, there are voices that used to sing with us, which we can no longer hear. But they will seem very close, and there will be no tears in our eyes. We will be reminding ourselves that our daughter and her husband will arrive on Christmas morning. And this year, for the first time, they will bring our grandson, nine months old.

We like Christmas Eve best. In the air of expectancy, touched by wonder, we live, for that evening, in the real world—which lies, mysterious, at the heart of life.

But Christmas morning is fine too. First we will go to church. I am the child of a minister, and church is home to me. I have made it part and parcel of my life; I go when I am discouraged, sick, frightened; I go when I am grateful and happy. But church on Christmas morning is special and very holy, for the Birth was the beginning of Christianity—the one second chance for the world. I pray that in the year to come I can be more worthy; and I give thanks for all the year has held since last Christmas, good and bad. I want, before I leave church on Christmas, to look squarely at that "bad" and see it for its worth, so I may profit by it in my soul.

After the early church service, we will all sit on the floor, beside the tree. We will open our presents in turn, each one opening while the others watch. And if our son-in-law tries to open out of turn, our daughter will say firmly, "Remember, on Christmas we do things as we have always done them. There are customs in this house!"

I tell this story because it will happen, not only to us, but to families everywhere, all over this great country, in December. In a world that seems to be not only changing but dissolving, there are tens of millions of us who want Christmas to be the same—with the old greeting, "Merry Christmas," and no other; with the abiding love among men of goodwill which the season brings. We hold fast to our customs and traditions at Christmas, whatever they may be, because they strengthen our family ties, bind us to our friends, and make us one with all mankind for whom the child was born.

So, in December, the old cry goes out, "Oh, come, all ye faithful." And we—the faithful, humble in the glory of the Incarnation—do not say that we "spend" Christmas, or "pass" Christmas. We "keep" Christmas: In all the years to come, we must continue, passionately, to keep it. For the spirit of Christmas is the hope of the world.

The Year We Had a "Sensible" Christmas

HENRY APPERS

December 1964

For as long as I could remember, our family had talked about a sensible Christmas. Every year, my mother would limp home from shopping or she would sit beside the kitchen table after hours of baking, close her eyes, catch her breath, and say, "This is the last time I'm going to exhaust myself with all this holiday fuss. Next year we're going to have a sensible Christmas."

And always my father, if he was within earshot, would agree. "It's not worth the time and expense."

While we were kids, my sister, Lizzie, and I lived in dread that Mom and Dad would go through with their rash vows of a reduced Christmas. But if they ever did, we reasoned, there were several things about Christmas that we, ourselves, would like to amend. And two of these were, namely, my mother's Uncle Lloyd and his wife, Aunt Amelia.

Many a time Lizzie and I wondered why families had to have

relatives, and especially why it was our fate to inherit Uncle Lloyd and Aunt Amelia. They were a sour and formal pair who came to us every Christmas, bringing Lizzie and me handkerchiefs as gifts and expecting in return silence, respect, service, and for me to surrender my bedroom.

Lizzie and I had understood early that Great-uncle Lloyd was, indeed, a poor man, and we were sympathetic to this. But we dared to think that even poverty provided no permit for them to be stiff and aloof and a nuisance in the bargain. Still, we accepted Great-uncle Lloyd and Great-aunt Amelia as our lot, and they were, for years, as much a part of the tradition of Christmas as mistletoe.

Then came my first year in college. It must have been some perverse reaction to my being away, but Mom started it. This was to be the year of the sensible Christmas. "By not exhausting ourselves with all the folderol," she wrote me, "we'll at last have the energy and the time to appreciate Christmas."

Dad, as usual, went along with Mom, but added his own touch. We were not to spend more than a dollar for each of our gifts to one another. "For once," Dad said, "we'll worry about the thought behind the gift, and not about its price."

It was I who suggested that our sensible Christmas be limited to the immediate family, just the four of us. The motion was carried. Mom wrote a gracious letter to Great-uncle Lloyd explaining that, what with my being away in school and for one reason and another, we weren't going to do much about Christmas, so maybe they would enjoy it more if they didn't make their usual great effort to come. Dad enclosed a check, an unexpected boon.

I arrived home from college that Christmas wondering what to expect. A wreath on the front door provided a fitting nod to the season. There was a Christmas tree in the living room, and I must admit that, at first, it made my heart twinge. The tree, artificial, was small and seemed without character when compared to the luxurious, forest-smelling firs of former years. But the more I looked at it, with our brightly wrapped dollar gifts under it, the friendlier it became; and I began to think of the mess of real trees, and their fire threat, and how ridiculous, how really unnatural it was to bring a living tree inside a house anyway. Already the idea of a sensible Christmas was getting to me.

On Christmas Eve, Mom cooked a good but simple dinner; and afterward we all sat together in the living room. "This is nice," Lizzie purred, snuggled in a big chair.

"Yes," Dad agreed. "It's quiet. I'm not tired out. For once, I think I can stay awake until church."

"If this were last Christmas," I reminded Mom, "you'd still be in the kitchen with your hours of 'last-minute' jobs. More cookies. More fruitcake." I recalled the compulsive way I used to nibble at Mom's fruitcake. "But I never really liked it," I confessed with a laugh.

"I didn't know that," Mom said. She was thoughtful for a moment. Then her face brightened. "But Aunt Amelia—how she adored it!"

"Maybe she was just being nice," Lizzie said undiplomatically.

Then we fell silent. Gradually we took to reading. Dad did slip off into a short snooze before church.

Christmas morning we slept late; and, once up, we breakfasted before advancing to our gifts. And what a time we had with those! We laughed merrily at our own originality and cleverness. I gave Mom a cluster-pin that I had fashioned out of aluminum measuring spoons and had adorned with rhinestones. Mother wore the pin all day or, at least, until we went out to Dempsey's.

At Dempsey's, the best restaurant in town, we had a wonderful, unrushed feast. There was only one awkward moment, just after the consommé was served. We started to lift our spoons; then Dad suggested that we say grace. We all started to hold hands around the table as we always do at home, but we hesitated and drew our hands back. And then, in unison, we refused to be intimidated by a public eating place and held hands and said grace.

Nothing much happened the rest of the day. In the evening I wandered into the kitchen, opened the refrigerator, poked around for a minute, closed the door, and came back to the living room.

"That's a joke," I reported, with no idea at all of the effect my next remark would have. "I went out to pick at the turkey."

In tones that had no color, Mother spoke. "I knew that's what you went out there for. I've been waiting for it to happen."

No longer could she stay the sobs that now burst forth from her. "Kate!" Dad cried, rushing to her.

"Forgive me. Forgive me," Mom kept muttering.

"For what, dear? Please tell us."

"For this terrible, dreadful, sensible Christmas."

Each of us knew what she meant. Our Christmas had been as artificial as that Christmas tree; at some point the spirit of the day had just quietly crept away from us. In our efforts at common sense, we had lost the reason for Christmas and had forgotten about others; this denied him whose birthday it was all about. Each of us, we knew full well, had contributed to this selfishness, but Mom was taking the blame.

As her sobs became sniffles and our assurances began to take effect, Mom addressed us more coherently, in Mom's own special incoherent way. "I should have been in the kitchen last night instead of wasting my time," she began, covering up her sentimentality with anger. "So you don't like my fruitcake, Harry? Too bad. Aunt Amelia really adores it! And Elizabeth, even if she doesn't, you shouldn't be disrespectful to the old soul. Do you know who else loves my fruitcake? Mrs. Donegan down the street loves it. And she didn't get her gift from me this year. Why? Because we're being sensible." Then Mom turned on Dad, wagging her finger at him. "We can't afford to save on Christmas, Lewis! It shuts off the heart."

That seemed to sum it up.

Lizzie had another way of saying it. She put it in a letter to me at school, a letter as lovely as Lizzie herself. "Mom feels," Lizzie wrote, "that the strains and stresses are the birth pangs of Christmas. So do I. I'm certain that it is out of our efforts and tiredness and turmoil that some sudden, quiet, shining, priceless thing occurs each year and if all we produce is a feeling as long as a flicker, it is worth the bother."

Just as my family came to call that "The Christmas That Never Was," the next one became "The Prodigal Christmas." It was the most festive, and the most frazzling time in our family's history—not because we spent any more money, but because we threw all of ourselves into the joy of Christmas. In the woods at the edge of town, we cut the largest tree we'd ever had. Lizzie and I swathed the house in greens. Delicious smells came from the kitchen as Mom baked and baked and baked. We laughed and sang carols and joked. Even that dour pair, Great-uncle Lloyd and Great-aunt Amelia, were almost, but not quite, gay. Still, it was through them that I felt that quick surge of warmth, that glorious "feeling as long as a flicker," that made Christmas meaningful.

We had just sat down in our own dining room and had reached out our hands to one another for our circle of grace. When I took Great-aunt Amelia's hand in mine, it happened. I learned something about her and giving that, without this Christmas, I might never have known.

The hand that I held was cold. I became aware of how gnarled her fingers were, how years of agonizing arthritis had twisted them. Only then did I think of the handkerchiefs that Lizzie and I had received this year, as in all the years before. For the first time I saw clearly the delicate embroidery, the painstaking needlework—Great-aunt Amelia's yearly gift of love to, and for, us.

At Christmas the Heart Goes Home

MARJORIE HOLMES

December 1976

t Christmas all roads lead home. The filled planes, packed trains, and overflowing buses all speak eloquently of a single destination: home. Despite the crowding and the crushing, the delays, the confusion, we clutch our bright packages and beam our anticipation. We are like birds driven by an instinct we only faintly understand—the hunger to be with our own people.

If we are already snug by our own fireside surrounded by growing children, or awaiting the return of older ones who are away, then the heart takes a side trip. In memory we journey back to the Christmases of long ago. Once again we are curled into quivering balls of excitement, listening to the mysterious rustle of tissue paper and the tinkle of untold treasures as parents perform their magic on Christmas Eve. Or we recall the special Christmases that are like little landmarks in the life of a family.

One memory is particularly dear to me—a Christmas during the Great Depression when Dad was out of work and the rest of us were scattered, struggling to get through school or simply to survive. My sister Gwen and her schoolteacher husband, on his first job in another state, were expecting their first baby. My brother Harold, an aspiring actor, was traveling with a road show. I was a senior working my way through a small college five hundred miles away. My boss had offered me fifty dollars—a fortune!—just to keep the office open the two weeks he and his wife would be gone.

"And boy, do I need the money! Mom, I know you'll understand," I wrote.

I wasn't prepared for her brave if wistful reply. The other kids couldn't make it either! Except for my kid brother Barney, she and Dad would be alone. "This house is going to seem empty, but don't worry—we'll be okay."

I did worry, though. Our first Christmas apart! And as the carols drifted up the stairs, as the corridors rang with the laughter and chatter of other girls packing up to leave, my misery deepened.

Then one night when the dorm was almost empty I had a long-distance call. "Gwen!" I gasped. "What's wrong?" (Long-distance usually meant an emergency back in those days.)

"Listen, Leon's got a new generator and we think the old jalopy can make it home. I've wired Harold—if he can meet us halfway, he can ride with us. But don't tell the folks; we want to surprise them. Marj, you've just got to come too."

"But I haven't got a dime for presents!"

"Neither have we. Cut up a catalog and bring pictures of all the goodies you'd buy if you could—and will someday!"

"I could do that, Gwen. But I just can't leave here now."

When we hung up I reached for the scissors. Furs and perfume. Wrist watches, clothes, cars—how all of us longed to lavish beautiful things on those we loved. Well, at least I could mail mine home—with IOUs.

I was still dreaming over this "wish list" when I was called to the phone again. It was my boss, saying he'd decided to close the office after all. My heart leaped up, for if it wasn't too late to catch a ride as far as Fort Dodge with the girl down the hall . . . ! I ran to pound on her door.

They already had a load, she said—but if I was willing to sit on somebody's lap. . . . Her dad was downstairs waiting. I threw things into a suitcase, then rammed a hand down the torn lining of my coat sleeve so fast it emerged mittened and I had to start over.

It was snowing as we piled into that heaterless car. We drove all night with the side curtains flapping, singing and hugging each other to keep warm. Not minding—how could we? We were going home!

"Marj!" Mother stood at the door clutching her robe about her, silver-black hair spilling down her back, eyes large with alarm, then incredulous joy. "Oh . . . Marj."

I'll never forget those eyes or the feel of her arms around me, so soft and warm after the bitter cold. My feet felt frozen after that all-night drive, but they warmed up as my parents fed me and put me to bed. And when I woke up hours later, it was to the jangle of sleigh bells Dad hung on the door each year, and voices—my kid brother shouting, "Harold! Gwen!" The clamor of astonished greetings, the laughter, the kissing, the questions. And we all gathered around the kitchen table the way we used to, recounting our adventures.

"I had to hitchhike clear to Peoria," my older brother scolded merrily. "Me, the leading man . . ." He lifted an elegant two-toned shoe—with a flapping sole—"in these!"

"But by golly, you got here." Dad's chubby face was beaming. Then suddenly he broke down—Dad, who never cried. "We're together!"

Together. The best present we could give one another, we realized. All of us. Just being here in the old house where we'd shared so many Christmases. No gift on our lavish lists, if they could materialize, could equal that.

In most Christmases since that memorable one, we've been lucky. During the years our children were growing up there were no separations. Then one year, appallingly, history repeated itself. For valid reasons, not a single faraway child could get home. Worse, my husband had flown to Florida to perform some vital surgery. A proud, brave man—he was adamant about our not coming with him "just because it's Christmas," when he'd be back in another week.

Like my mother before me, I still had one lone chick left—Melanie, fourteen. "We'll get along fine," she said, trying to cheer me.

We built a big fire every evening, went to church, wrapped presents, pretended. But the ache in our hearts kept swelling. And, the day before Christmas, we burst into mutual tears. "Mommy, it's just not right for Daddy to be down there alone!"

"I know it." Praying for a miracle, I ran to the telephone. The airlines were hopeless, but there was one roomette available on the last train to Miami. Almost hysterical with relief, we threw things into bags.

And what a Christmas Eve! Excited as conspirators, we cuddled together in that cozy space. Melanie hung a tiny wreath in the window and we settled down to watch the endless pageantry flashing by to the rhythmic clicking song of the rails: little villages and city streets, all dancing with lights and decorations and sparkling Christmas trees; and cars and snowy countryside and people—all the people—each one on his or her special pilgrimage of love and celebration this precious night.

At last we drifted off to sleep. But hours later I awoke to a strange stillness. The train had stopped. And, raising the shade, I peered out on a very small town, silent, deserted, with only a few lights still burning. And under the bare branches, along a lonely street, a figure was walking—a young man in sailor blues, head bent, hunched under the weight of the sea bag on his shoulders. And I thought, *Home! Poor kid, he's almost home.* And I wondered if there was someone still up waiting for him; or if anyone knew he was coming at all. And my heart cried out to him, for he was suddenly my own son—and my own ghost, and the soul of us all—driven, so immutably driven by this annual call, "Come home!"

Home for Christmas. There must be some deep psychological reason why we turn so instinctively toward home at this special time. Perhaps we are acting out the ancient story of a man and a woman and a coming child, plodding along with their donkey toward their destination. It was necessary for Joseph, the earthly father, to go home to be taxed. Each male had to return to the city of his birth.

The tremendous miracle of birth shines through every step and syllable of the Bible story. The long, arduous trip across the mountains of Galilee and Judea was also the journey of a life toward birth. Mary was already in labor when they arrived in Bethlehem, so near the time of her delivery that in desperation, since the inn was full, her husband settled for a humble stable.

The child who was born on that first Christmas grew up to be a man, Jesus. He healed many people, taught us many important things. But the message that has left the most lasting impression and given the most hope and comfort is this: that we do have a home to go to, and there will be an ultimate homecoming, to a place where we will indeed be reunited with those we love.

Anyway, that's my idea of heaven. A place where Mother is standing in the door, probably bossing Dad the way she used to about the turkey or the tree, and he's enjoying every minute of it. And old friends and neighbors are streaming in and out, and the sense of love and joy and celebration will go on forever.

A place where every day will be Christmas, with everybody there together. At home.

His Mysterious Ways

"NO HOT CHOCOLATE on Christmas Eve?" our teenage daughter, Christine, asked.

I looked away. "Next year," I promised as she went to get ready for the midnight service.

We'd always had hot chocolate on Christmas Eve; it was a tradition. But this year we couldn't afford even that simple item. When my husband, Jack, had been laid off six months earlier, he had started a claims-adjusting business, working out of our basement. But the response had been dreadful, and it didn't help when our car's transmission died. Our older daughter, Janice, contributed her earnings from her first full-time job, and the girls never complained about doing without. Still, as the year drew to a close, our financial picture looked bleaker and bleaker.

As we headed out the door, my eyes fell on our old artificial tree, draped with last year's dulled tinsel. *And I couldn't even squeeze money for hot chocolate out of our budget*, I thought. During the service, I prayed silently, *Oh, Lord, you promised to take care of us. Have you forgotten?*

Everyone except me, it seemed, was uplifted by the message of hope in the service. At its close, people hugged and shook hands. As we bundled up in coats and scarves, Christine's youth counselor called to us: "Wait!" She pulled a ribboned jar from her bag. "Merry Christmas." She had brought us hot chocolate mix!

She hadn't known about our family tradition. And she didn't know that, to me, this simple gift was a reminder that God had not forgotten us after all.

—CHERYL MORRISON, *December 1994*

Homemade Holy Night

Ella Ruth Rettig

December 1982

Where did I get the idea of a family Christmas pageant? I don't really know. All I can say is that when the idea came to me, I felt that I might never see a Christmas again.

It was June. I had just gone through major cancer surgery that wasn't fully successful. Once a month I would travel 250 miles to Houston for chemotherapy; and returning home, I felt sick to death.

The days were long. My husband, Gene, is a telephone repairman, and we live on a hilltop in the farm country of central Texas. It's beautiful country, but I had no energy to go out in it. I'd just sit by the window and watch our horse loping from the barn to the shade of the mulberry tree. I'd lost my appetite and my hair, but, worst of all, at times I was too sick to care whether or not I got well.

My family tried to bolster my spirits, but I couldn't seem to focus on anything. Then I tried playing a little game with myself.

"Get rid of all those gloomy thoughts, Ella Ruth," I told myself. "Start thinking only good, bright thoughts." And when I asked myself what was good and bright, I came up with Christmas, my favorite time of year.

If only, I thought, *If only I could feel that every day was leading me nearer and nearer to Christmas.*

But what could I do? Start my Christmas shopping early, in the summer? No, that would be silly. Well, maybe I could plan a special celebration that would bring my family all together. And of course it should honor Jesus' birth. I had read somewhere that cancer patients should set goals; a Christ-honoring Christmas became one of my goals.

What I really wanted to do was bring the Christmas story to life for my grandchildren. Maybe a Christmas play . . .

Yes! But how? Where? With what? My mind and body were weak. How could I put a play together?

I prayed, "Father, I want to honor you, but you'll have to show me how. I don't even know where to start."

Slowly God got me going. Looking out the window, I saw our barn and thought, *There! There's the manger, Ella Ruth.*

I knew what the plot of the play should be—it was right there in Luke.

Then I wondered who in my family could play what parts. Right away I saw that we had a perfect Mary—my daughter Kristi was pregnant, due in February. And her husband Bobby had a beard. He could be Joseph. The angels and shepherds? My grandchildren.

There was my cast. But what would we do? Stand around in

the barn? No. Somehow I would have to come up with a simple script, and so I studied Luke 2 and Christmas books for ideas.

And costumes. Did I have the needed strength to make them? I really didn't want anybody's help. I wanted this to be a secret between the Lord and me.

"Go slow," I heard God saying, "and I'll help you." I did take it slow. During my long afternoons, I would sit beside our old cedar trunk, rummaging through mementoes of wonderful times.

There was an old jeweled collar . . . how stylish I'd felt wearing this in the long-ago days when my husband and I were courting. Now the collar could be a Wise Man's crown. A red and black afghan . . . here was a labor of love. My daughter Kristi had made this for me just before her marriage. Now it could keep warm a king of the Orient. Old elastic hairbands and old towels—sewn together they'd make headdresses for the shepherds.

My house took on new life, with all the objects in it calling out to be used.

One day, though, while turning a pillowcase into a shepherd's dress, I suddenly suffered doubts. Was I setting myself up for a big embarrassment? What if my children and grandchildren thought this was a stupid, silly idea? Would six-year-old Jeremy take one look at his pillowcase and say, "Forget it"?

But the longer I thought, the more sure I was that my family—they were all a bunch of "actors," anyway—would play along wholeheartedly. So I hoped.

A month before the holiday, I let my husband Gene in on my secret. I needed him to make the "star in the East" and shepherds' crooks in his workshop. And when we made the drive to Houston for my chemotherapy, the fear and silence were a little less terrible. Gene and I had pageant details to talk about.

Then, before I knew it, the holiday was upon us; I arranged to have all of our family gather at our house for Christmas Eve. They suspected something when I told them to wear warm clothes.

All was going well until the day before, when a heavy rain began to fall. Would we be able to get to the manger in the barn? I forlornly painted a king's crown, and looked up now and then to see the rain come pouring down.

The morning of Christmas Eve, though, we woke up to a clear sky and a brisk north wind. By noon, the way to the manger was dry.

During Christmas Eve dinner, I was a bundle of joyous nerves. I could barely eat. As everyone began the after-dinner cleanup, Gene and I exchanged winks and then he slipped outside to set up the star and arrange things in the barn.

Dishes done, everyone gathered around me, waiting for me to spill my secret. But my doubts were back. Would everyone try to back out? Handing out costumes and printed instructions, I didn't dare look up to see how everyone was reacting. But then my son Mike quietly said, "Hey, Ma, I haven't seen you this excited since . . . in a long time."

I felt I'd just been given a big dose of bravery. When everyone was dressed, I began to read from Luke 2 and the pageant at last began to unfold. Joseph and Mary ("being great with child") left the house and I told of their journey to Bethlehem. With no room at the inn, they took refuge in the barn. We then watched from the window as shepherds went out into the field. My daughter-in-law Donna wore an old quilt top and a towel headdress, and her little Jeremy and Kerrie wore old pillowcases.

Then "the angel of the Lord" (my oldest grandchild) "came upon them." Tracy was wrapped in a white bedsheet, with a tinsel halo nestled in her hair. I flipped a light switch and "the glory of the Lord shone round about them." More angels, little Kellie (Kerrie's twin sister) and Stephanie, appeared. The angels brought "good tidings of great joy" to the shepherds, and then they all headed for the manger. I followed, leaving the Wise Men in the house.

In the barn everything was dark, except for a gentle glow shining on Mary, Joseph, and the Babe (a doll) in swaddling clothes. Angels and shepherds and my husband kneeled or stood in the shadows, silent in the cold night air.

I stood at the door and read the story of the Wise Men from Matthew 2. My husband's handmade "star in the East," a flashlight hidden within a cardboard star, began moving along its cable toward the barn. The Wise Men (my two sons, Ron and Mike, and our family friend David Taylor) followed the star across the field, singing "We Three Kings of Orient Are."

And then the Wise Men were with us, in their jeweled and (bath-) robed splendor, presenting their gifts as an angel sang "Silent Night." Then the grandchildren sang "Away in a Manger." We all joined in on "Joy to the World."

This was all I had planned. But none of us could move. We all felt God's warm presence in this cold, dark barn.

My oldest son Ron gently broke the stillness, saying, "I feel like we should pray." Ron led us in a prayer of praise, and we then sang another carol, and then another, all of us wanting to hang on a little longer to this loving closeness.

And in that closeness I no longer felt like the sick one in the family. I simply felt like one of the family—a good loving family. I'd left my fear behind. My soul was full of light, a newborn light that God had been leading me to for six months. It was the radiance of the manger, a radiance I'd helped God create.

So you see, if you're stricken by illness or misfortune, set some goals. Find something worthwhile to do. And then do it. Make a Christmas pageant or an Easter vigil or organize a bake sale. If you know a trade, offer your services to those in need. To get better, you often have to go out of your way. Don't be afraid. Go.

It *Is* a Wonderful Life

JIMMY STEWART

December 1987

A friend told me recently that seeing a movie I made more than forty years ago is a holiday tradition in his family, "like putting up the Christmas tree." That movie is *It's a Wonderful Life*, and out of all the eighty films I've made, it's my favorite. But it has an odd history.

When the war was over in 1945, I came back home to California from three years of service in the Air Force. I had been away from the film business, my MGM contract had run out, and frankly, not knowing how to get started again, I was just a little bit scared. Hank Fonda was in the same boat, and we sort of wandered around together, talking, flying kites and stuff. But nothing much was happening.

Then one day Frank Capra phoned me. The great director had also been away in the service, making the *Why We Fight* documentary series for the military, and he admitted to being a little frightened too. But he had a movie in mind. We met in his office to talk about it.

He said the idea came from a Christmas story written by Philip Van Doren Stem. Stem couldn't sell the story anywhere, but he finally had two hundred twenty-four-page pamphlets printed up at his own expense, and he sent them to his friends as a greeting card.

"Now listen," Frank began hesitantly. He seemed a little embarrassed about what he was going to say. "The story starts in heaven, and it's sort of the Lord telling somebody to go down to earth because there's a fellow who's in trouble, and this heavenly being goes to a small town, and . . ."

Frank swallowed and took a deep breath. "Well, what it boils down to is, this fella who thinks he's a failure in life jumps off a bridge. The Lord sends down an angel named Clarence, who hasn't earned his wings yet, and Clarence jumps into the water to save the guy. But the angel can't swim, so the guy has to save him, and then . . ."

Frank stopped and wiped his brow. "This doesn't tell very well, does it?"

I jumped up. "Frank, if you want to do a picture about a guy who jumps off a bridge and an angel named Clarence who hasn't won his wings yet coming down to save him, well, I'm your man!"

Production of *It's a Wonderful Life* started April 15, 1946, and from the beginning there was a certain something special about the film. Even the set was special. Two months had been spent creating the town of Bedford Falls, New York. For the winter scenes, the special-effects department invented a new kind of realistic snow instead of using the traditional white cornflakes. As one of the longest American movie sets ever made until then, Bedford

Falls had seventy-five stores and buildings on four acres with a three-block main street lined with twenty full-grown oak trees.

As I walked down that shady street the morning we started work, it reminded me of my hometown, Indiana, Pennsylvania. I almost expected to hear the bells of the Presbyterian church, where Mother played the organ and Dad sang in the choir. I chuckled, remembering how the fire siren would go off, and Dad, a volunteer fireman, would slip out of the choir loft. If it was a false alarm, Dad would sneak back and sort of give a nod to everyone to assure them that none of their houses was in danger.

I remembered how, after I got started in pictures, Dad, who'd come to California for a visit, asked, "Where do you go to church around here?"

"Well," I stammered, "I haven't been going—there's none around here."

Dad disappeared and came back with four men. "You must not have looked very hard, Jim," he said, "because there's a Presbyterian church just three blocks from here, and these are the elders. They're building a new building now, and I told them you were a movie star and you would help them." And so Brentwood Presbyterian was the first church I belonged to out here.

Later, that church was the one in which Gloria and I were married. A few years after that, it was the same church I'd slip into during the day when Gloria was near death after our twin girls were born. Then after we moved, we attended Beverly Hills Presbyterian, a church we could walk to.

It wasn't the elaborate movie set, however, that made *It's a Wonderful Life* so different; much of it was the story. The character I played was George Bailey, an ordinary kind of fella who thinks he's never accomplished anything in life. His dreams of becoming a famous architect, of traveling the world and living adventurously, have not been fulfilled. Instead he feels trapped in a humdrum job in a small town. And when faced with a crisis in which he feels he has failed everyone, he breaks under the strain and flees to the bridge. That's when his guardian angel, Clarence, comes down on Christmas Eve to show him what his community would be like without him. The angel takes him back through his life to show how ordinary, everyday efforts are really big achievements.

Clarence reveals how George Bailey's loyalty to his job at the building-and-loan office has saved families and homes, how his little kindnesses have changed the lives of others, and how the ripples of his love spread through the world, helping make it a better place.

As good as the script was, there was still something else about the movie that made it different. It's hard to explain. I, for one, had things happen to me during the filming that never happened in any other picture I've made.

In one scene, for example, George Bailey is faced with unjust criminal charges and, not knowing where to turn, ends up in a little roadside restaurant. He is unaware that most of the people in town are arduously praying for him. In this scene, at the lowest point in George Bailey's life, Frank Capra was shooting a long shot of me slumped in despair. In agony I raise my eyes and, following the script, plead, "God . . . God . . . dear Father in heaven, I'm not a praying man, but if you're up there and you can hear me, show me the way. I'm at the end of my rope. Show me the way, God. . . ."

As I said those words, I felt the loneliness, the hopelessness of people who had nowhere to turn, and my eyes filled with tears. I broke down sobbing. This was not planned at all, but the power of that prayer, the realization that our Father in heaven is there to help the hopeless, had reduced me to tears.

Frank, who loved spontaneity in his films, was ecstatic. He wanted a close-up of me saying that prayer, but was sensitive enough to know that my breaking down was real and that repeating it in another take was unlikely. But Frank got his close-up anyway.

The following week he worked long hours in the film laboratory, again and again enlarging the frames of that scene so that eventually it would appear as a close-up on the screen. I believe nothing like this had ever been done before. It involved thousands of individual enlargements and extra time and money. But he felt it was worth it.

There was a growing excitement among all of us as we worked day and night through the early summer of 1946. We threw everything we had into our work. Finally, after three months and shooting some sixty-eight miles of 35-millimeter film, we completed the filming and had a big wrap-up party for everyone. It was an outdoor picnic with three-legged races and burlap-bag sprints, just like the picnics back home in Pennsylvania.

At the outing, Frank talked enthusiastically about the picture. He felt that the film as well as the actors would be up for Academy Awards. Both of us wanted it to win, not only because we believed in its message, but also for the reassurance we needed in this time of starting over.

But life doesn't always work out the way we want it to.

The movie came out in December 1946, and from the beginning we could tell it was not going to be the success we'd hoped for. The critics had mixed reactions. Some liked it ("a human drama of essential truth"); others felt it "too sentimental . . . a figment of simple Pollyanna platitudes."

As more reviews came out, our hopes sank lower and lower. During early February 1947, eight other current films including *Sinbad the Sailor* and Betty Grable's *The Shocking Miss Pilgrim*, outranked it in box-office income. The postwar public seemed to prefer lighthearted fare. At the end of 1947, *It's a Wonderful Life* ranked twenty-seventh in earnings among the other releases that season.

And although it earned several Oscar nominations, and despite our high hopes, it won nothing. Best picture for 1946 went to *The Best Years of Our Lives*. By the end of 1947, the film was quietly put on the shelf.

But a curious thing happened. The movie simply refused to stay on the shelf. Those who loved it loved it a lot, and they must have told others. They wouldn't let it die any more than the angel Clarence would let George Bailey die. When it began to be shown on television, a whole new audience fell in love with it.

Today, after some forty years, I've heard the film called "an American cultural phenomenon." Well, maybe so, but it seems to me there is nothing phenomenal about the movie itself. It's simply about an ordinary man who discovers that living each ordinary day honorably, with faith in God and a selfless concern for others, can make for a truly wonderful life.

Silent Night in Burma

LEE ADAIR LAWRENCE

December 1997

When I was twenty-two, knowing I would not be home for Christmas had a strange effect on me: I swelled with pride. After college I had worked in Japan, then backpacked around the globe. The plan had been to make it home to Atlanta by Christmas. Yet there I was on December 20 landing in Burma instead.

I can forgo the tree and presents, I told myself as I boarded a crowded bus. I could survive without the familiar preparations: Mother perched on the big bed, the phone nestled between shoulder and ear, calling unmarried cousins and widowed aunts, inviting all the "strays" to Christmas dinner. . . . Father seated at the kitchen table jotting down the groceries we needed to get at the store.

The previous year, Daddy and I had spearheaded the dinner effort. With no real concern for proportions we chopped tart apples, celery, onions, garlic, and pecans, and scraped them into a bowl for stuffing, wondering aloud whether to add more pecans or to defer to my mother's healthy eating habits. A mischievous grin crinkled Daddy's face as he reached for the bag of pecans. "Merry Christmas," he said.

This year will be different, I thought. *Curry instead of turkey, bamboo instead of pine*. Burma was a Buddhist country, after all. *No Christmas here*. I smiled smugly, as though doing without the rituals was evidence of my maturity.

On the flight I had met Sue, an English girl with short black hair and milky skin, and we had decided to tour Burma together. Over the next four days we made our way to Pagan, the ancient capital, crowded with brick and stucco shrines. There we found a clean, sparsely furnished room under a thatched roof. The rest of the hotel was rented to eight Burmese policemen and their chief; the jolly owner indicated in fractured English that two girls alone could not ask for better protection.

That evening we ate noodles at one of the restaurants in town, telling each other that it was just another day and we didn't need to be home with our families simply because it was Christmas Eve. We walked back to the hotel under a brilliant full moon. Lingering in the common room, I chatted with the chief policeman, who was sitting in one of the two wicker armchairs. He had an athletic build and a face that was easy to trust. When he said in slightly accented English that he was taking his crew to one of the ancient temples and there was room for us, I didn't hesitate.

In an open truck Sue and I sat on benches among the policemen. The chief had pinned the flaps back so we could look out onto a landscape dotted with ancient shrines made otherworldly by the moon's platinum light.

When the truck stopped, we hopped out. The Ananda Temple rose before us. Its white stucco walls gleamed like marble, and the spire shimmered, making me think of church steeples back home. We left our shoes in the truck and walked barefoot through an arched entryway. Sue and I followed the chief, walking clockwise around the central spire, as prescribed by Buddhist tradition. He brought his hands together and bowed deeply at each shrine. When finished he turned to us and said, "It is your Christmas Eve, isn't it?"

"Yes," Sue and I whispered.

Then to our surprise, he began to sing: "Silent night, holy night . . ."

We joined in, only to find he knew more verses than either of us! As we made our way down the marble-white walkway, its smooth surface cool under our bare feet, I thought of my father whistling in the kitchen. Before I could check them, other images rushed in: Daddy carving the turkey, Mother giving the silver serving spoons a last-minute shine, my two brothers herding relatives into the living room to show them our tree.

How could I have fooled myself? I missed them terribly. Tears filled my eyes and trickled down my cheeks. The chief segued into "The First Noel," and I appreciated his effort to make us feel at home. It was beautiful, and peaceful, and I thought of the first Christmas. Wasn't that what made my family's rituals so powerful?

At the white arch the chief stopped. He spread his arms wide as though to embrace the ghostly beauty of his moonlit temple. "Merry Christmas," he said, grinning widely.

I smiled back. I was still fiercely homesick, but also, in some mysterious way, home was with me. It wasn't the tree, or the presents under it, or the turkey stuffing. It was something inside me, wherever I went.

Sue and I hugged, then turned to the chief to hug him. But he deflected our Western display of affection by pressing his hands together and bowing. We took his lead and greeted him in kind, wishing him a very merry Christmas.

Our Family Tree

CHRISTOPHER RADKO

December 2001

*H*oliday music streamed from the speakers in the department store that December day in 1984. I was twenty-four years old and struggling to make it on my own, but I still couldn't resist getting swept up in the excitement of the season. It helped subdue the worry I felt about the future and what I was going to do with my life. After graduating from Columbia University with a degree in English, I'd gotten a job in the mailroom of a talent agency. I was making a paltry salary. A couple of years later, I felt none too enthusiastic about the "real world."

I was in the store that day getting supplies for my family's Christmas. A part of me wished I were a kid again. Back then, I had spent my time lying under the sea-green branches of our Christmas tree, daydreaming. Our house had cathedral ceilings, so we always got the tallest tree we could find, usually a fourteen-foot noble fir. I'd look up into the branches at the hundreds of antique, hand-blown glass ornaments Grandmother

Veronica had brought with her when she came to America from Poland as a young woman, family treasures that her mother and grandmother had passed down. There were stars and comets, kites and parasols, candy canes and icicles, a Santa in a basket under a hot-air balloon, a crèche, and a flurry of angels. I wasn't supposed to touch them because they were fragile, so I just looked at them wonderingly.

Once I'd gotten older, I was allowed to help set up and decorate the tree. Now that I was working, I had money to get a tree stand. The old cast-iron one we'd used for years was covered with so much sap and grime, I couldn't get it clean.

At home that night we decorated the tree. "I'll never forget the day Mama surprised me with this," Grandmother Veronica said in her warm, rich accent, holding up a glass bird. "All my friends used to make faces in this one," she said, pointing to a large mirrored ball. Listening to Grandmother tell the story behind each ornament, I almost felt as though the people from the Old Country she described—who were as dear to her as she was to us—were there too.

We finished, and my family went to get ready for dinner while I got the vacuum cleaner to remove some of the fallen needles. I was in the hallway when I heard a tremendous crash. I dropped the vacuum and raced back into the living room. I gasped. The tree had fallen over! Thousands of glass fragments glittered all over the carpet.

In a moment the rest of the family was at my side—including Grandmother, sobbing. I was the one who discovered why the tree had fallen over, and in one agonizingly long moment I realized it was all my fault. A leg of the new tree stand I'd put up had collapsed. I forced myself to turn and face Grandmother, who met my eyes. She didn't have to say it—I had ruined Christmas forever.

Almost every ornament had shattered or cracked when the tree fell. Amid the debris I spied a tiny unicorn Grandmother had given me when I was a boy. "For little Christopher with the big imagination," she had said. I picked it up and turned it over in my hands. It was completely undamaged, right down to the slender glass horn. My first instinct was to run and show it to Grandmother. But then I stopped myself. *What about all the other ones that are lost forever?* I thought. *Your foolishness has destroyed the family tree.*

Promising to replace the ornaments, I went back to the store where I'd been a few days earlier. Nearly every ornament was plastic or cheap metal. The few glass pieces were obviously mass-produced. I scrounged the city, but everything had been picked over. We put the tree back in the old iron stand, tied it to the wall, and hung some dried flowers along with the few surviving glass ornaments. Every time I walked through the living room, seeing that sparsely covered tree reminded me of my guilt. At midnight Mass I could barely meet Grandmother's eyes. I couldn't wait for Christmas to be over.

After the holidays I plodded on with my job, not knowing any better what to pursue careerwise than I knew how to make amends for what I'd done. I felt down for months. Some time in the spring I got a letter from my cousin, Margaret, in Poland. "Heard about what happened at Christmas," it read. "Why don't you come visit for Easter?"

I thought a change of scene would help lift my spirits and

also maybe I would be able to find something for Grandmother in the Old Country. I took my vacation time and flew to Poland.

When I got there I told Margaret all about my fruitless search for blown-glass ornaments. "I have an idea," she said. She led me to an apothecary's window and pointed at some hand-blown, prismatic laboratory vials, tubes, and beakers. They were surprisingly beautiful. "I went to high school with the glass blower," she said. "Maybe he can help."

We went to a small garage-like building to talk to Margaret's friend. He took off his black-rimmed glasses and polished them as I described the globes, reflectors, angels, and icicles I wanted.

"Do you think you could sketch some of the designs?" he asked me.

"I'm not sure," I said. "I can try." I sat down at his worktable and closed my eyes. Could this be the chance I'd prayed for? I so wanted to make things right. In my mind I imagined holding the delicate old ornaments as I scouted the right spot for them on the tree. I made a few tentative strokes on the pad. Slowly the pencil seemed to take on a power of its own. The designs flowed onto the paper—icicles with tapering ends, globes with concave mirrors, stars with tiny moons painted on them.

The glass blower examined my designs with a perplexed expression. "These are the kind of ornaments my grandfather used to make before the war. Nobody wants these old things any more."

"Oh, we do," I said. "They're what made our tree special. Can you make them?"

He shrugged. "I'll do my best."

I spent the rest of the week seeing the sights with my cousin, wondering how the ornaments would come out. I came back to the shop and was presented with a large box. I opened it and caught my breath. Inside lay eighteen delicate hand-blown glass ornaments, just like the ones that had broken. The craftsman had silvered each on the inside and his wife had painted them iridescent colors. I picked up a silver ball and held it in front of me, my face reflected in it.

"I don't know how to thank you," I said finally. "These are exactly like the ones Grandmother used to have."

"Well, all I did was make them the way you drew them. Enjoy."

The whole flight back to America, I couldn't stop thinking of the ornaments. I'd never dreamed I'd be able to get such perfect replacements! I imagined the look on my Grandmother's face when she saw them.

In the meantime I took the ornaments to work to show them off. My coworkers were awed. "How much do you want for 'em?" one asked. Another promised to top the first guy's offer. For me it was more than a whole day's pay at my job. *Maybe I can cable Margaret some money and order more ornaments*, I thought. *I might actually be able to pay my rent on time for a change.*

When I showed the ornaments to Grandmother, her eyes grew wide. "Where did you find these?" I explained how I'd gotten them made in the Old Country just for her. Grandmother picked up an ornament and cradled it in her hand. "It's heavy, just like the old ones. And so shiny!"

When a box of glittering ornaments from Poland arrived at my workplace, my coworkers bought them all that same day. During my lunch hour I found myself doodling new designs on a napkin. A friend suggested I try selling the ornaments at a local gift store. Figuring the money would come in handy for buying more ornaments, I gave it a try. I didn't have an appointment, but when the secretary for the store buyer saw the ornaments I'd brought, she picked up the phone. "Sir," she said, "there's a guy here with something I think you'll like."

They gave me a huge order. I maxed out my credit card to purchase ornaments through Margaret. I also sent her my new designs. I fulfilled my shipment to the gift store and loaded the extras into the trunk of my beat-up Oldsmobile. I went from store to store selling them. Then I sent samples and photos to buyers for stores. It was a lot of trial and error. Maybe one in ten stores I contacted said yes.

All my free time was spent packing and shipping the ornaments that arrived from Margaret, and designing new ones. I'd gone beyond just recreating the broken ones and started putting in some twists of my own. In one year's time, I sold twice my salary's worth of ornaments! Still I hesitated to quit my job. But after selling quadruple the amount the second year, it was "Goodbye, mailroom. Hello, Christmas!" I started my own company, employing skilled craftsmen from all over Eastern Europe to produce beautiful, finely detailed ornaments based on my designs.

Perhaps people like my ornaments because they sense in them the same link to the past that I do. For me, a Christmas tree is like a family diary. I like to imagine that years after I'm gone, someone decorating their tree will pick up one of my ornaments and say, "Look, this one belonged to my great-great-grandmother. It dates all the way back to 2001!"

The best part for me was getting the chance to help Grandmother rebuild her collection before she passed away in 1995. The last Christmas we spent together we reminisced over old times as we hung new hand-blown glass ornaments I'd designed on our family tree. Near the center I placed the unicorn that had been spared all those years before. Little had I known at that time how blessed I would be in turning a tragedy into a success. "I hope that all of these new ornaments are at least a fraction as precious to you as this one is to me," I said to my grandmother.

"Oh, Chris," she said, patting my cheek. "I'm so very proud of you." I hugged her tight and together we gazed at the ornaments hanging on the family tree in a sparkling confluence of light and color, present and past—and once again, anything seemed possible.

A Season of Forgiveness

The Kidnapping
in Victory Church

THE EDITORS

December 1947

*E*arly on Christmas morning, 1933, the Pastor of Our Lady of Victory Church in San Francisco was interrupted at his morning prayers. His sexton was in such turmoil he could barely speak, and behind him the young curate was pale and wide-eyed.

"I've just opened the church, Father, and found the Infant, Father—the Christ Child is gone! Gone from the manger-crib!"

"That's absurd!" The old priest rose to his feet as he looked disbelievingly from one to the other. He strode with some exasperation down the rectory stairs and into the church. The first Mass of the day, at six that morning, was barely a half hour away. What kind of panic would sweep through the parish when the people found the Christ Child gone?

Even before he had verified the disappearance for himself, the priest's thoughts were concerned with the thief. What kind of fiend—what infidel—would so outrage a shrine? Was this perpetrated by someone who wished to defile and desecrate the symbol of the very birth of Christianity? Or was it for revenge on the priest, the congregation, or upon God and his Church?

"Shall we call the police, father?" the Curate asked.

The old priest shook his head. He glanced about the church he loved and which only four and a half hours ago had been filled with the happiest crowds of the year, the attendees of midnight Mass. He wanted no scandal to touch his church. He walked away silently.

Back in the rectory he got into his overcoat and rubbers. The streets were clean with snow. Already the early crowd was coming to church, and he greeted those he passed with a hearty "Merry Christmas" he did not feel. As he reached a corner, a small boy, running as he pulled an express wagon, almost knocked him down.

"Georgie Potter!" the priest began, indignantly, but at the sight of the upturned ruddy shining little face of the seven-year-old, he sighed and smiled. "Now, is that a new wagon I see?"

"Yes, Father!"

"You're up early enough to get your presents, I must say." Suddenly the priest stiffened. "Georgie! What—is—that—in—your wagon?"

The Christ Child! The priest stared transfixed. The beloved statuette of the Infant Jesus with its baby arms outstretched in wide benediction lay with a blanket tucked about it!

The shining light was gone from the child's face and he cowered.

"Georgie—did you take that from the church?"

"But I promised, Father!" the boy blurted defensively. "I prayed and prayed for a red wagon. And I promised the Christ Child if he'd get me a red wagon for Christmas, I'd give him a ride in it twice around the block."

In One Blinding Moment

MAX ELLERBUSCH

December 1960

*I*t was a busy Friday, six days before Christmas, 1958. I was in my instrument-repair shop, working feverishly so that I could have all of the Christmas holiday at home with my family. Then the phone rang and a voice was saying that our five-year-old Craig had been hit by a car.

There was a crowd standing around him by the time I got there, but they stepped back for me. Craig was lying in the middle of the road; his curly blond hair was not even rumpled.

He died at Children's Hospital that afternoon.

There were many witnesses. It had happened at the school crossing. They told us that Craig had waited on the curb until the safety-patrol boy signaled him to cross. *Craig, how well you remembered! How often your mother called after you as you started off for kindergarten, "Don't cross till you get the signal!" You didn't forget!*

The signal came; Craig stepped into the street. The car came so fast no one had seen it. The patrol boy shouted, waved, had to jump for his own life. The car never stopped.

Grace and I drove home from the hospital through the Christmas-lighted streets, not believing what had happened to us. It wasn't until that night, passing the unused bed, that I knew. Suddenly I was crying, not just for that empty bed, but for the emptiness, the senselessness, of life itself. All night long, with Grace awake beside me, I searched what I knew of life for some hint of a loving God at work in it, and found none.

As a child I certainly had been led to expect none. My father used to say that in all his childhood he did not experience one act of charity or Christian kindness. Father was an orphan, growing up in nineteenth-century Germany, a supposedly Christian land. Orphans were rented out to farmers as machines are rented today, and treated with far less consideration. He grew into a stern, brooding man who looked upon life as an unassisted journey to the grave.

He married another orphan and, as their own children started to come, they decided to emigrate to America. Father got a job aboard a ship; in New York harbor he went ashore and simply kept going. He stopped in Cincinnati, where so many Germans were then settling. He took every job he could find, and in a year and a half he had saved enough money to send for his family.

On the boat coming over, two of my sisters contracted scarlet fever; they died on Ellis Island. Something in Mother died with them, for from that day on she showed no affection for any living being. I grew up in a silent house, without laughter, without faith.

Later, in my own married life, I was determined not to allow these grim shadows to fall on our own children. Grace and I had four: Diane, Michael, Craig and Ruth Carol. It was Craig, even more than the others, who seemed to lay low my childhood pessimism, to tell me that the world was a wonderful and purposeful place. As a baby he would smile so delightedly at everyone he saw that there was always a little group around his carriage. When we went visiting it was Craig, three years old, who would run to the hostess to say, "You have a lovely house!" When he received a gift he would be touched to tears, and then he would give it away to the first child who envied it. Sunday mornings when Grace dressed to sing in the choir, it was Craig who never forgot to say, "You're beautiful."

And if such a child can die, I thought as I fought my bed that Friday night, *if such a life can be snuffed out in a minute, then life is meaningless and faith in God is self-delusion.* By morning my hopelessness and helplessness had found a target—a blinding hatred for the person who had done this to us. That morning police picked him up in Tennessee: George Williams. Fifteen years old.

He came from a broken home, police learned. His mother worked a night shift and slept during the day. Friday he had cut school, taken her car keys while she was asleep, sped down a street. . . . All my rage at a senseless universe seemed to focus on the name George Williams. I phoned our lawyer and begged him to prosecute Williams to the limit. "Get him tried as an adult—juvenile court's not tough enough."

This was my frame of mind when the thing occurred which changed my life. I cannot explain it; I can only describe it.

It happened in the space of time that it takes to walk two steps. It was late Saturday night. I was pacing the hall outside our bedroom, my head in my hands. I felt sick and dizzy, and tired, so tired. "Oh God," I prayed, "show me why!"

Right then, between that step and the next, my life was changed. The breath went out of me in a great sigh—and with it all the sickness. In its place was a feeling of love and joy so strong it was almost pain.

Other men have called it "the presence of Christ." I'd known the phrase, of course, but I'd thought it was some abstract, theological idea. I never dreamed it was Someone, an actual Person, filling that narrow hall with love.

It was the suddenness of it that dazed me. It was like a lightning strike that turned out to be the dawn. I stood blinking in an unfamiliar light. Vengefulness, grief, hate, anger—it was not that I struggled to be rid of them, but like goblins imagined in the dark, in morning's light they simply were not there.

And all the while I had the extraordinary feeling that I was two people. I had another self, a self that was millions of miles from that hall, learning things men don't yet have words to express. I have tried so often to remember the things I knew then; but the learning seemed to take place in a mind apart from the one I ordinarily think with, as though the answer to my question was too vast for my small intellect. But in that mind beyond logic, that question was answered. In that instant I knew why Craig had to leave us. Though I had no visual sensation, I knew afterward that I had met him, and he was wiser than I, so that I was the little boy and he the man. And he was so busy. Craig had so much to do, unimaginably important things into which I must not inquire. My concerns were still on earth.

In the clarity of that moment it came to me: this life is a simple thing! I remember the very words in which the thought came. "Life is a grade in school; in this grade we must learn only one lesson: we must establish relationships of love."

Oh, Craig, I thought. *Little Craig, in your five short years how fast you learned, how quickly you progressed, how soon you graduated!*

I don't know how long I stood there in the hall. Perhaps it was no time at all as we ordinarily measure things. Grace was sitting up in bed when I reached the door of our room. Not reading, not doing anything, just looking straight ahead of her as she had much of the time since Friday afternoon.

Even my appearance must have changed, because as she turned her eyes slowly to me she gave a little gasp and sat up straighter. I started to talk, words tumbling over each other, laughing, eager, trying to say that the world was not an accident, that life meant something, that earthly tragedy was not the end, that all around our incompleteness was a universe of purpose, that the purpose was good beyond our furthest hopes.

"Tonight," I told her, "Craig is beyond needing us. Someone else needs us—George Williams. It's almost Christmas. Maybe, at the juvenile detention home, there'll be no Christmas gift for him unless we send it."

Grace listened, silent, unmoving, staring at me. Suddenly she burst into tears.

"Yes," she said. "That's right, that's right. It's the first thing that's been right since Craig died."

And it has been right. George turned out to be an intelligent, confused, desperately lonely boy, needing a father as much as I needed a son. He got his gift, Christmas Day, and his mother got a box of Grace's good Christmas cookies. We asked for and got his release, a few days later, and this house became his second home. He works with me in the shop after school, joins us for meals around the kitchen table, is a big brother for Diane and Michael and Ruth Carol.

But more was changed, in that moment when I met Christ, than just my feelings about George. That meeting has affected every phase of my life, my approach to business, to friends, to strangers. I don't mean I've been able to sustain the ecstacy of that moment; I doubt that the human body could contain such joy for very many days.

But I now know with certainty that no matter what life does to us in the future, I will never again touch the rock-bottom of despair. No matter how profound the blow seems, the joy I glimpsed that blinding moment when the door swung wide is even more profound.

Prodigal Father

DALE KUGLER JR.

December 1972

At seventy-three, Marcia Pollock's father was a man of great independence, a man of great pride. He had been an ironworker, a career that gave him great satisfaction, even looking back. He loved to point out to his grandchildren the construction jobs he had worked on—the huge advertising structures in Times Square, some of New York's mightiest bridges. The kids called him "Poppy," a contagious name that everybody used.

Poppy lived in a furnished room in his old neighborhood, and he had a job, part-time, at Baltz's Pharmacy. After Marcia's mother died, Poppy had firmly and flatly refused Marcia and Jack's invitation to come live with them. He was stubborn about not intruding on their lives, about not crowding their little house, about not becoming a burden.

Yet the truth of the matter was that they really wanted him. Poppy was good to be around. He was always on the up side, always helpful. The kids loved him because he listened to them and worked with them and because, too, he always brought them something. There were always special gifts on birthdays and at Christmas. And whether it was a little bunch of bachelor buttons for Marcia, or a new after-shave from Baltz's for Jack, Poppy simply never arrived empty-handed.

And so it was with shock and bewilderment that Marcia went to see Poppy in the hospital that summer. He had collapsed in the street. The doctors told Marcia that Poppy had been living on coffee and doughnuts.

"Why, Poppy, why?" Marcia wanted to know. "There's no reason to go without food. You have money. You have us. . . ." But Poppy just brushed the whole subject aside.

"You're wrong," Otto Baltz told Marcia later that day. "He has practically no money at all—just the government check and what little he makes here. Yet I myself saw him spend most of his last check on your little boy's bicycle."

She became stern with Poppy. "You're foolish, Poppy," she said.

"I have my pride," Poppy answered.

"False pride," she hurled back at him.

During the autumn, Poppy didn't come around as often as he had in the past; but when he did, he would still arrive with little gifts in hand. And he would look at Marcia with a defiance she had never seen in him.

"I can't come over Christmas Day," Poppy told her just before the holidays. "This year I promised I'd watch the store."

Marcia knew Baltz's was not open on Christmas.

From then on she grew more distressed with each day that

passed. She had to do something, but she floundered until the morning she sat down and wrote a letter.

> Poppy dear,
> This will be brief. We'll miss you at Christmas, all of us, because you are one of us. I am praying for you—as always.
>
> And, Poppy, lately I've been thinking about the parable of the prodigal son and its meaning for Christians, especially in the confusion of Christmas. What's more important in that situation, the destruction of pride—or the triumph of love?
> We love you.
> Marcia

All Christmas morning Marcia thought about Poppy.

Half an hour before the turkey went on the table, the doorbell rang. Marcia jumped. She knew it was Poppy.

The kids rushed to him and in their great surprise inundated Poppy with more hugs and kisses than he had ever had before. Poppy then looked at Marcia. Now there was no defiance in his eyes, only snap and sparkle like the Poppy of old. Yet there was something else, a look of triumph, the look of a battle won.

Poppy held out his arms to Marcia, and his hands, those strong ironworker's hands, were empty, utterly empty—yet never had they been more filled.

His Mysterious Ways

ON CHRISTMAS DAY a young man, tall and slim with dark hair, was making his way south on Interstate 85 just below High Point, North Carolina, trying to hitch a ride.

For two years he hadn't been home; his family had heard nothing from him. He and his mother had had a disagreement, and he had set off across the country, going from town to town, from odd job to odd job. He worked at filling stations and produce markets; he drove a taxi and picked crops; he was an orderly in a nursing home and a plumber's assistant. But now he was ready to go home.

He had only thirty miles to go, but a ride was hard to find. "Mom," he said to himself, "I'm tired and hungry, but I'm coming home."

The cold wind blew and a few trucks rumbled by. Then, from across the road, he heard a voice call his name. "Mike! Hey, Mike, come here!" To his surprise, there was his stepfather, waving, calling to him from his truck. Mike ran across the highway. "Get in, Son. We're going home."

Mike tossed his bag in the back of the truck and embraced his stepfather. "Fred," he said, "how did you happen to be here?"

"I came to pick you up," Fred said, amazement in his voice. "Drove straight here."

"But how did you know I'd be here? I didn't write. I didn't call."

"Your mother sent me. Just this morning in her prayers for you, she knew you were coming and that you were on I-85 just below High Point."

The two men looked at each other without saying a word. Then Fred started the motor. "She's waiting for you, Son."

—FRED NICHOLAS (MIKE'S STEPFATHER), *December 1989*

The Girl from Across the Sea

ELLEN PORTER

December 1980

*I*n late August, Mitsuyo came to live with my family in California as a high-school exchange student from Japan. She was eighteen, two years older than my daughter Jennifer, who was to be her American "sister" for the year.

The first letter we received from Mitsuyo's father, a business-man in a small town just outside Tokyo, said, "Eat her what you eat." He had written in a small, neat hand, struggling with our difficult and unfamiliar language. "Correct her as your daughter when she needs to correct. For my daughter is willful. . . ."

My husband and I smiled at the phrasing, but I thought I sensed what Mitsuyo's parents must be feeling. It took great trust to allow their only daughter to come to a faraway country to live among strangers. I vowed to treat Mitsuyo with special kindness.

I thought her father overly modest in his assessment of Mitsuyo's character. During the first few weeks, she showed no sign of willfulness. On the contrary, she showed no sign of indi-viduality at all. Day after day she went to school with Jennifer, wearing those childish middy blouses of which she had a great number. Night after night she sat at dinner watching us from beneath brows that were rule-straight, not arched as Jennifer's were. She ate what we ate. She seemed neither happy nor unhappy; she expressed no opinions.

Effusively I tried to make her feel like a welcome guest in our house, but she seemed reserved and unresponsive. Of course, her English was poor at first, and trying to communicate was a great effort. Gradually it became easier not to try.

For weeks things went on quietly, Mitsuyo fading more and more into the background. But as it turned out, the quietness was all on the surface.

"Just look at this!" I complained one Saturday as I tried to finish the cleaning. "Both of you girls have left your beds unmade again!" I stared exasperatedly around the room the girls shared, as I started immediately fixing Mitsuyo's bed.

"Mom, where's my new blouse?" was Jennifer's only response, from the depths of the closet. "I can't find it anywhere! And I have to meet Jerry in ten minutes."

I wasn't sympathetic. "It's your fault for not keeping your room neater," I said. "Weren't you looking for your tennis shorts last week? And a T-shirt the week before? I certainly don't have time to keep up with your things for you! Get busy fixing up around here, young lady."

Jennifer chose another blouse and dashed away, still grumbling. I sighed and connected the vacuum cleaner. Quickly I vacuumed around Mitsuyo's bed and picked up. I left Jennifer's half of the room as it was.

Mitsuyo watched me quietly for a while and then took her homework and silently left the room.

Well, I thought, Mitsuyo could be excused for not understanding, or for imitating Jennifer's bad example.

That afternoon I missed the china dog that usually sat on the mantelpiece. It was only a cheap souvenir; still I was annoyed. I remembered that Mitsuyo had been alone in the living room a good part of the afternoon. And I remembered Jennifer's repeated searches for one item of clothing or another. Suddenly, I was suspicious.

I found Mitsuyo and asked about the dog. She denied seeing it; but I thought there was a shifty look in her eyes.

Monday, when the girls were in school, I cold-bloodedly searched Mitsuyo's belongings—all except her suitcase, which I couldn't open. I found nothing. I should have confronted her about the situation, but I was too embarrassed to admit what I'd done.

From that time, I began watching Mitsuyo. As I did so, I discovered that I didn't really like having this silent foreigner in our midst; especially now that I suspected her of being untrustworthy. But I said nothing of my suspicions to anyone except my husband, James. He said I should be more patient.

In December I agreed to be chairman of decorations for our church Christmas party. It was a big job. I was responsible for making hundreds of small Nativity figures out of felt, pipe cleaners, and dime-store jewels. The Holy Family, the Wise Men, the animals—all the figures were to decorate the hall and the

Christmas tree for the party a week before Christmas. Then the decorations were to be sold, with the money going to the church.

My dining room became a workshop, with church members coming now and then to help with the project. Mitsuyo tried to help, but couldn't seem to get things right. Her figures were rather crudely made. Neither James nor Jennifer was interested in helping. Jennifer, in fact, had recently acquired a new boyfriend who occupied most of her attention, leaving Mitsuyo to fend for herself.

But time was short; and, since I had so much to do, my temper became short also.

Only Mitsuyo and I were in the house the day I counted the figures I had made that morning and found that some were missing. At last I exploded. That girl! I'd had enough of her sly ways!

I stormed into her room without so much as knocking. There, sure enough, were my sheep and cow, my Mary and Joseph and Baby Jesus that Mitsuyo had stolen from the dining room. She was in the act of placing them in her suitcase, which was unlocked and open on her bed. I shoved her away and looked at the collection of things in the suitcase: Jennifer's pink blouse, her T-shirt, tennis shorts, and my china dog. And other things—a sweater, scarves, handkerchiefs, even a table napkin—that no one had missed.

Mitsuyo was sitting wide-eyed on the bed. I grabbed a handful of things from the suitcase and shook them under her nose. I shouted, "Is this the way you thank us for having you here? Is it? You little thief! I'm tired of this, and I'm getting you out of my house right now!"

I ran downstairs, flung the handful of stolen figurines on the kitchen table and rummaged through the desk looking for the phone number of the district representative of the exchange student organization. Wait until he heard what that innocent-looking girl had been up to! Wait until her parents found out, and all her friends. She'd be sent home in disgrace, and it would serve her right!

I found the number and sat with my hand on the telephone. I was seething with such anger that for a moment I didn't trust myself to speak. Over the months, my resentment must have built up more than I realized. I fought to calm myself, to phrase what I would say to the representative so that I would sound reasonable and detached, not hurt and vindictive. As my breathing became quieter, I heard hoarse sobs from the bedroom upstairs. *She ought to cry!* I thought.

Then my glance fell on the untidy heap on the kitchen table. *What in the world could have possessed that strange girl to steal this worthless collection of things?* On top of the pink blouse were the figures of Mary, Joseph, and the Baby Jesus, a little white bundle with a tiny brown head and sleeping eyes.

Why had she stolen my Holy Family? Upstairs the heartbroken cries continued. Did she miss her own family? I gazed at the little figure of Jesus, an emblem of he who came to bring forgiveness to the world.

Perhaps I should at least go up and ask her why she had done it. In all her months with us, I realized I had not really come to know her.

I climbed the stairs, feeling that perhaps I had been too harsh; and when I saw the small, sobbing figure lying on the bed, I was almost moved to tears myself. I went to her and touched her, putting my arm halfway around her shoulder, and to my surprise she threw herself into my arms weeping like a child. Her dark, straight hair fell over my shoulder.

"Why did you take these things, Mitsuyo? They're worthless."

In halting English, between sobs, she said, "I was not to keep them. I only hold with me for a while because they were something of you."

It hit me like a shock wave. I had given her everything—food, shelter, gifts—everything but myself. She wanted some part of each of us that we had withheld from her—our love.

"Always," she sobbed, "you made my bed. You didn't talk to me as you did to Jennifer!"

To me she had always been the foreigner—someone whom first I treated as a guest, then as a culprit, never as a member of the family.

Now all her hurts and fears spilled out. She'd been self-conscious at school because the other students thought her clothes were strange. She'd wanted so much to be one of us—just for a little while—that she'd taken our things as a symbol of us, taken them as a security blanket for the love she was missing.

I dried her tears. I told her that I understood. "I'll forgive you," I said, "if you'll forgive me." And she laid her head against my cheek.

The church Christmas party was a great success. Jennifer's romance had blown away a few days before, and the three women in the family had a hilarious time making Wise Men and sheep and Holy Families. Who was to criticize if some were crudely made? We are all crudely made—we are not perfect. Just forgiven.

The Kidnapped Doll

MYRTLE "COOKIE" POTTER

December 1994

The family was gathered on Christmas Eve at my grand-parents' house in San Francisco. I was six that year, and my cousin Tom was eight. We'd waited for months, and now that the time for gift-giving was almost near, every moment seemed a lifetime. Would I get the baby doll I longed for—the one in the window of Mrs. O'Connor's variety store? For months I'd spent part of every day staring at her with my nose pressed against the pane. I was certain that baby doll looked sad every time I left.

"Why don't they give out the presents right now?" I asked. "Why do we have to wait until after dinner?"

"I can't wait," said Tom. "Let's sneak into the living room. Maybe we can find out what we're getting."

"Grandpa and the uncles are out in the garden," I said. And our cousins Dorothy, Mildred, and Mabel were in the attic playing dress-up.

We peeked in the kitchen. The aroma of fresh-baked bread and roasting turkey with sage dressing filled the air. Grandma smiled as she chopped onions. Aunt Agnes and Aunt Susan bumped happily against each other as they stirred the gravy. But Aunt Margaret scowled as she basted the turkey. "You can't come in here," she said, shaking her spoon at us.

So far so good. Everyone was accounted for. We hurried down the hall to the front of the house and cautiously turned the knob on the living-room door. My heart beat fast. This was forbidden territory until after dinner. We each took a deep breath, and Tom pushed the door open.

What a sight! The magnificent pine tree, aglow with lights of every color, was covered with tinsel and bright ornaments. On the top an angel rested serenely, his sparkling wings brushing the ceiling.

"Wow," whispered Tom. "Look at the presents." The rug was covered with gifts. He fell to the floor and started to shake the boxes that bore his name. "This one's just clothes, I think, but doesn't this one sound like an erector set?"

I was too busy to answer. One of my packages smelled like perfume, another like chocolate. But where was a box that might hold a baby doll? I glanced around the room and spied something covered with a quilt behind a couch. I rushed to it and lifted the cover. Underneath was a buggy—with a doll inside. "My baby!" I cried, picking her up and hugging her.

"Put her back," hissed Tom, yanking my arm. "That doll's not yours. See, the tag says 'To Dorothy.'"

I refused to look. "She's mine," I insisted, jerking away. "I've wanted her forever. Santa just made a mistake putting Dorothy's name on her."

Clutching the doll, I ran down the hall and out the back door to Grandpa's workshop. Quickly I thrust the baby onto a pile of wood shavings behind a stack of lumber.

Tom came storming in after me. "You're a kidnapper and a thief," he cried. Then, losing interest, he announced he was going inside. I ran behind him. Tom's last remark worried me: "Do you think you're the only one who wanted a doll? Dorothy asked Santa for a baby too."

I hadn't thought of that. What if it really was hers? Her parents would be upset that the doll was missing. Tom would tell on me. Mama would be ashamed. Aunt Margaret would stare down her nose at me, just like her stuck-up daughter Dorothy.

If that doll was Dorothy's I'd never hear the end of it. Why had I taken her? I had to put her back. My heart beating wildly, I ran as fast as I could to Grandpa's workshop and was about to open the door when I heard voices. Grandpa was in there showing Uncle Edward the cabinet he was building. I couldn't go in now.

Just then Grandma called us to dinner. Shakily I climbed the steps to the house.

In the dining room we bowed our heads as Grandpa said grace. "We thank you, Lord," he began, "for letting us all be together on the day of Jesus' birth." I almost choked. It was bad enough to be a thief and a kidnapper, but to think I'd done it all on Baby Jesus' birthday!

After that I had no appetite. When our mothers finally

cleared the table and started to do the dishes, I hurried back to the workshop, hoping I could get the doll. But Grandpa was in there again, this time with Uncle Archie.

When we finally gathered in the living room, my face felt hot. The party dress Mama had made me seemed too tight around my neck.

Grandpa began calling names and giving out presents. He waited for each person to open the gift before he called another name. I stole a look at Tom; he was totally involved in unwrapping his own packages. After an hour, Dorothy's buggy was still behind the couch. Though I'd received several presents, Mama could see I wasn't happy. She left the room and came back wheeling a doll buggy. "Santa left this for Myrtle," she said.

I gasped. Inside was a doll better than the one I'd taken. She had a different dress, a pretty bonnet, and a coverlet of pink and blue satin. She wore a ruffled petticoat, lace panties, and booties. I knew Mama had made them; the blanket was of the same satin she'd used to make Grandma a robe. My baby was so special that I hugged her tightly and vowed never to let her go.

Suddenly I felt sick to my stomach. For a moment I'd forgotten Dorothy's doll. It was still missing.

"What's the matter, Myrtle," said Mama. "Don't you like her?"

"Oh, Mama, I love her."

But of course I couldn't enjoy my present until I put Dorothy's doll back. How could I possibly do it? *Jesus!* It was his birthday. Maybe he could help me. *Jesus*, I prayed silently, *I'm sorry I was so bad. Please help me make things right.*

Grandpa called for attention. "We've got a lot more presents to give out. But we're going to take a recess. Pumpkin pie with whipped cream is waiting in the dining room."

This was my chance! As everyone headed for dessert, I stole out the back door and down the steps. This time no one was in the workshop. Behind the lumber, with her dress askew and wood shavings in her hair, lay Dorothy's doll. I grabbed her and got her back to the living room without being seen. I picked the shavings out of her hair, smoothed her clothes, and started to put her in the buggy behind the couch.

But my heart sank when I saw a pink smear on her cheek. Grandpa painted landscapes, and there must have been a drop of paint on the wood shavings. Rub as I might, I couldn't get it off. Dorothy and Aunt Margaret would be sure to notice it.

I knew what I had to do. With trembling fingers I undressed both dolls. I put Dorothy's doll clothes on my perfect doll, and the clothes Mama had made on the doll with the smudged cheek. I put the perfect doll in Dorothy's buggy and the one I'd kidnapped in my buggy with her smeared cheek against the pillow.

When everyone returned to the living room, Grandpa finished giving out the presents. Dorothy received her doll and was just as happy with her as I had been.

"Our dolls look like twins," I said. "Let's have a tea party for them."

"That'll be fun," said Dorothy. "I'll bring cookies."

She's not stuck-up, I told myself. *I'm sure we can be friends.*

"Mama," I said that night as I was getting into bed, "I'm naming my doll Mary, after Jesus' mother."

"That's lovely," said Mama. "You know, your doll has a little pink mark on her cheek. Mrs. O'Connor has a lot of other dolls in her store. I'm sure we can exchange her."

"No," I cried. "I like her just the way she is."

I snuggled in my blanket, holding Mary close, filled with an overwhelming joy that had nothing to do with dolls or buggies. I was only six years old, but already I'd sensed it: When you do something bad, it's possible, with God's help, to make things right.

Moment of Grace

PETER ROCKWELL

December 2001

*G*rowing up in Norman Rockwell's household wasn't quite as idyllic as the *Saturday Evening Post* illustrations he was famous for. You see, my father's work consumed him. He was at his easel painting every day of the year, including holidays. Even on Christmas, after we opened presents, he retreated to his studio.

Many people knew my father's art well. All I knew was that he was always working. Being Norman Rockwell was such a huge undertaking that it didn't leave time for being a father. His art meant everything to him. Sometimes he'd ask me what I thought of the painting he was working on. "It's great, Pop. The best one ever," I would say, because that's what he needed to hear. Once he had me pose for a *Post* cover. It was a blistering-hot day in August 1946, and I had to sit in a railroad car without air conditioning for hours so he could get it just right.

"What's the big deal?" I complained. "It's just a painting."

My father's eyes widened a bit as if he were amazed I could even think something like that. "Peter, a painting is so much more than lines and color on a canvas," he said. "It can bring people together, show them what's most important. A painting is an idea come to life. Do you understand?"

I didn't. Not really. I mean, his art sure didn't bring us together.

I went to boarding school, then college, where many people regarded my father's work with disdain. They dismissed as irrelevant the values his art embraced. Believe it or not, I was embarrassed by what my father had come to stand for. So I distanced myself from his world, instead throwing myself into studying and sports, especially fencing.

During one match, my opponent's épée broke and the blade pierced my lungs and heart. I nearly died.

As I recovered I took a fresh look at my life. I knew it had taken a power greater than science to save me after the fencing accident, and that knowledge humbled me. I found myself appreciating little things so much more—the texture of a tree trunk, the line of a bird's wing, the shape of someone's face. I ended up in a sculpting class. I loved watching the clay transform beneath my hands. I became a sculptor and started doing work for parks and churches.

Though my work—both stylistically and thematically—was far different from his, my father came to support my career. I had my own family, with four kids to raise. Sometimes when we were on camping trips, I'd feel a pang of regret that I didn't have those kinds of memories with my own father. When he passed away in the late 1970s, that sense of sadness deepened. It was strange to be identified with someone to whom I had so much trouble relating.

Then, in 1994, I was contacted by the Institute for the Study of the Middle and Far East to lend my expertise to researchers excavating ancient stone carvings in the Swat Valley in northern Pakistan. Working with an international team of researchers amid the towering mountains, I was struck by the contrast with the everyday American life that was the realm of my father's work.

One night I was invited to dine at the home of a local Muslim doctor. The aroma of strong spices greeted me as I entered his home and pulled off my shoes. "I would like you to meet my daughter and daughter-in-law," the doctor said. I cast him a surprised look. I knew local custom was not to allow strangers to meet the women of a household.

"It would be an honor," I said. The doctor introduced me to two young women dressed in brightly colored clothes. One held a large book under her arm. "We are so pleased to meet you," she said to me. "Your father is our favorite artist." I saw then the book she held was a collection of his illustrations.

We sat down together as the women began leafing through the pages of the book. "This is great," one told me. It was *Saying Grace*, which depicts a grandmother and little boy in a crowded diner quietly praying over their meal.

I looked up at the two Pakistani women. "Why do you like it?" I asked.

"Because it's about giving thanks to the one who gave us life," the daughter said. "And about what it means to be a family," said the other. These women were from a different culture, different religion, different generation from my father, yet they had found something in his paintings that deeply resonated for them. *A painting is an idea come to life*, he had told me. And finally I understood. His ideas and his values were universal.

I wondered if I had been led to sculpting after my brush with death—and to this foreign family who cherished his work. Somehow, half a world from where he had lived and worked, I felt closer than ever to my father.

Interlaced

MARY FAITH RUSSELL

December 2003

*I*t was the week before Christmas, 1966, in Carvin, a small mining town in northern France. My husband, Bill, got transferred there to be a technical director for an American-owned plastics plant. We pulled up stakes and moved from Massachusetts with our three young children. At first it seemed a great adventure, but for me it quickly turned into a real adjustment. Bill, who spoke fluent French, fit right in. But I struggled with the language. I also found it hard to get used to the rigid social and class distinctions, so unlike the States.

Automobiles shared Carvin's streets with horse-drawn carts full of potatoes and sugar beets. Most folks walked. "Pardon," I said one morning, maneuvering among the townsfolk while carrying spears of bread called baguettes. I turned off the main thoroughfare and followed the street to our house. "Hi!" I called out, pushing the old door open. Bill was helping the children string lights on the evergreen tree we'd bought from a farmer. He came over and relieved me of the baguettes. "Did you visit the woman down the street?" he asked.

"No, just shopped," I said. The previous Sunday the pastor of our little church had drawn me aside. "I've heard there are newcomers on your block," he had said. "Madame Delplace and her husband and children have moved from Strasbourg. She could use a helping hand. Perhaps you could drop by?"

Drop by? I'd passed Madame Delplace one day on the narrow sidewalk in front of our houses. She carried herself proudly, and when I offered a timid *"Bonjour,"* she sailed past without a reply.

"Don't bother with her," a neighbor had called out from her window. "The husband has had trouble with the police."

"I can't just force myself on her," I told Bill. "I'm sure she won't talk to an American, much less one who speaks such patchy French."

Bill lifted our six-year-old so she could put the star on top of our tree. "Why not at least try?" he said.

The next day I walked down the block and knocked on Madame Delplace's door.

Madame Delplace answered, wearing a heavy black sweater, her hair pulled back in a bun and her lips pressed together tightly. *"Je suis Madame Russell,"* I said.

She hesitated, her gray eyes appraising me warily. I thought she might slam the door in my face. But she stepped back. *"Entrez, s'il vous plaît,"* she said. I quickly realized the reason for the sweater. Her house was freezing cold.

She motioned me to sit and brought me a cup of tea. The kettle hung over a small fireplace. "You are lucky to have come while the kettle is still hot," she said. "We have no money to buy coal. We've taken down the doors and burned them when we need to."

I listened intently and was able to follow what Madame said. "You see," she explained, "my husband did just one tiny thing wrong." She held up the tip of her little finger to show how small it was. "He broke a French business law and the government forced us into bankruptcy to pay his debt. Officials auctioned off all our possessions. The only things we could keep were a chair apiece and our mattresses."

She acted relieved to tell someone of her plight, a relief that seemed mixed with bitterness and pride. "We have a small social security stipend," she said. "Our only other income is from stringing beads for carnival jewelry. In one stroke," she said, "I went from being middle class to lower class. No one in this town will talk to me."

"Madame," I said, choosing my words carefully in French, "I will talk to you. And it would be my pleasure to bring you some things for Christmas. For your children."

She looked at me steadily, then nodded. "*Merci.*" She snipped the word off like one would snip the stem of a rose.

My kids were excited about giving presents to the Delplace kids. They picked out some of their own toys. We wrapped them and took them to Madame Delplace's house, along with an envelope containing seventy dollars in francs. "This is not money that is to be repaid," I said. "Someday you'll be able to pass the money on to someone else who needs it."

She clasped my hand. "You have saved us," she said, her voice wavering.

I visited Madame Delplace every week. One day Madame took out her needlework, a ball of thread and a hook. With a flick of her wrist she began crocheting.

"What are you making?" I asked.

She held up a circle of intricate flower designs, woven in shades of a warm, almost golden, beige. Her work was exquisite. "How beautiful!" I exclaimed.

"A tablecloth for my sister," Madame said. "Do you have a sister?"

"No," I replied. "Just one brother, back in the States."

"We miss them, no?" She looked up and smiled as if trying to cover up the sadness in her voice.

I loved my weekly teatime with Madame, not simply because my French was rapidly improving. We talked about serious subjects—politics, international affairs, religion. We discussed racism and injustice in both our countries. We agreed that God loves us all. "We are all the same in God's eyes," Madame Delplace said. Still, her words seemed to move upon a current of bitterness. There was something so unresolved in her passions, something deeper than her husband's shame. Each time her voice rose she seemed to pull her emotions back with her crocheting, her fingers pulling the hook more quickly.

The winter softened into spring. "Would your children like to come play with mine?" Madame asked. The playdate went so well that I invited her children to our house to watch television.

"Would you like these clothes?" I asked Madame Delplace in the summer, holding up some shirts my girls had outgrown. She nodded and offered to make some lemonade. At every teatime as we talked in the soft afternoon light, her crochet needle kept moving, transforming the ball of thread into a delicate cascade.

Before I knew it, it was only a week till Christmas. Holiday lights bloomed on lampposts. *Bûches de Noël*—rich cakes shaped like Yule logs—appeared in the patisseries. *This year has flown by, and I think I know why. Thank you, Lord, for sending me Madame Delplace. And, please, this Christmas bring peace to her troubled heart.*

The next time I went to Madame's for tea, sprigs of holly were arrayed over the fireplace. "I have finished the tablecloth," she announced.

"Please," I said, "I have to see."

Slowly, almost reverently, Madame Delplace spread the cloth over the kitchen table. I caught my breath. "This could go into a museum!" I whispered.

She did something unexpected then. She folded up her treasure and held it toward me. "It is for you," she said.

"I . . . I can't," I stammered. "You made it for your sister."

"You are my sister," she insisted. "In all of our times together this past year, there is one thing I have never spoken about. The war. American planes bombed Strasbourg. Those bombs killed my father. In my grief and rage I vowed I would always hate Americans. Then you came to visit me and to be my friend, and my bitterness melted. You must take this cloth as an expression of my thankfulness. Please."

I clasped the cloth close to me. "*Merci beaucoup,*" I whispered, feeling both forgiven and forgiving.

So many years now have passed. But those serious topics

Madame Delplace and I discussed over tea and crocheting still trouble the world. I think of the bitterness that divides people. Yet I remember her holding out that beautiful, exquisite cloth, so delicate and so strong, and I am reassured that there is hope for us all. I remember that Christmas in a faraway place where I found a sister.

The Joy of Giving

A New Look at Myself

DOROTHY HOPKINS

December 1960

*J*ust before the Christmas of 1939, my situation seemed impossible, or so I thought. I had a dull job with poor pay, and a despot for a boss; my dreary basement apartment in Chicago was shared with what I considered an ungrateful, unemployed sister; my ten-year-old daughter was beginning to show signs of being mentally disabled; my estranged husband completely ignored his obligations. I felt hopeless.

During the long, daily ride to work on the streetcar, I had developed a sort of mechanical habit of praying, as though God were a Santa Claus. I would pray for a raise in salary, but I hated my job and my boss. I would pray for help from my estranged husband, but I considered him a cheat, a liar, and a drunkard. I would pray for better living conditions, but I despised our apartment and monotonous "economical" food.

Then, on the very Friday before Christmas, the sky fell in. I lost my purse containing a week's salary! I was in a department store when I became aware that my purse was gone. It was closing time, and I had to rush to the store's office to report my loss and ask for carfare home.

Outside, on State Street, Christmas carols filled the air, but their beauty did not penetrate the bitterness in my heart. At that moment, I felt that Jesus Christ's mission on earth was all in vain.

By the time I got a seat on the streetcar, anger commenced to dissolve into self-pity. I began to pray again. "Why, God," I asked, "why did all these things have to happen to me?" Tears came to my eyes, and I had no handkerchief. I felt alone in a world without love.

Presently I felt something touch my hand. A woman sitting next to me was silently offering a handful of tissues. She didn't speak, and neither did I, but somehow I knew that she was also handing me compassion and understanding. Suddenly a wall seemed to give way inside of me and I felt ashamed.

I began to pray again, but this time with real humility. I prayed for forgiveness; I prayed for guidance; I prayed for understanding. And as I prayed, an amazing transformation took place in my attitude concerning the people toward whom I had felt so bitter earlier: My sister, suddenly, was an undeserving captive of my sharp criticism and morose outlook. I began to wonder if the relationship between my husband and myself might not have been different had I given more thought to his viewpoints, and less to my own problems.

For the first time, I began to associate my boss's disagreeableness with his struggle to keep the firm solvent against stiff competition. And for the first time in many months, I thought of my daughter as someone sweet, to be loved and cared for, rather than a constant source of worry and anxiety.

By the time I arrived home, being broke no longer seemed so important. I still had a job, a family to love and to love me, and a warm apartment. Many, many that night had less!

The next morning, a surprising succession of blessings started to reach us. First, two young schoolgirls delivered a large Christmas box of food. Soon after that, our insurance agent came by with word that I could convert my policy and receive a sizable cash settlement.

Also, in the next few days, I received a money order from my husband, and my unemployed sister secured work during the holidays.

To top it all, on the first of the year I was promoted to a much better job with a raise. My employer had been considering me for the promotion; but before my change he hadn't liked my negative attitude toward work.

Although this whole experience seemed to bring many material rewards, the most important benefit to me was discovering the kind of prayer where I quit trying to run my life and turned everything over to God. The result was that God gave me the desire to change myself, and at the same time he allowed me to view through his loving eyes all the wonderful people close to me.

I Was a Stranger

RICHARD A. MYERS

December 1963

Christmas can be an adventure for anyone who does not mind a little walking or meeting a few unpredictable situations. The adventure I had just before Christmas 1961 made it the most memorable of my life.

A reservist called back to duty during the Berlin crisis, I was at Fort Monmouth, New Jersey. An alert just before Christmas canceled out my plans to spend the holidays with my parents in Indiana.

Feeling low, I turned on the radio one morning and happened to catch an announcement: "The General Post Office in New York City would welcome volunteers who would like to answer the letters to Santa Claus which have piled up."

Did they mean in person?

It wasn't clear to me, but I was intrigued anyway. An overnight pass got me to New York on Saturday. With permission from a clerk in the dead-letter department of the postmaster general's office, I spent a couple of hours sorting and poring over letters to Santa which filled two huge hampers.

I selected four letters with New York addresses and debated whether to buy the toys the writers asked for. It seemed wiser to let events develop spontaneously. So, whistling "Santa Claus Is Coming to Town," I started out on my adventure.

The first address took me to Harlem and the apartment of Grace, who had written to Santa Claus on behalf of her four children. The door was opened by a clean-cut man of thirty-five. I explained about the letter to Santa Claus.

"You might call me a new kind of Santa's helper," I said.

Grace's husband was cordial, invited me in, and, since he was a recently discharged serviceman himself, we quickly struck up a friendship. Grace was away, but he introduced me to the children and we had a delightful visit. Reluctantly, he accepted a gift for the children.

My second letter was from Kathleen, with a request for toys for her and her sister, signed with many kisses for Santa. When I arrived outside her luxurious brownstone house with brass knobs and kick plates on the doors, I almost turned away. But I finally did knock. Kathleen's mother opened the door and, after hearing my story, called her daughter. "Santa Claus has sent his helper to see you," she explained.

With wide eyes, Kathleen sat down beside me while I explained to her about Christmas and assured her she would not be forgotten.

"Your visit has meant a lot to Kathleen," her mother said to me as I left. "We can give her toys but we can't always give her the joy of this kind of experience."

William, age ten, had written from a location in Spanish Harlem. I ended up in a filthy tenement but was unable to find the exact address. Instead, I found myself talking to a tired woman with five children. Impulsively, I handed her enough money to buy presents for all her brood.

The fourth letter was from Lucille, a young mother who wrote that she was separated from her husband, but she hoped that Santa would help her with gifts for her two little girls. When I rang the doorbell, a man answered.

Disconcerted, I tried to explain my mission. Lucille then appeared and invited me inside. "My husband and I are together again," she whispered to me happily.

As I told the couple of my experiences that day, we were soon laughing together in a spirit of friendship. "You see," I explained, "I am the one who is grateful. What better way could a lonely serviceman so enjoy a Christmas adventure?"

It was true. All day I had traveled about in subways and on buses. My feet were soaked from the snowy streets. There had been no spectacular experiences; several had been awkward. There had been only one case of real need. But for one whole day, I hadn't thought of myself once and had enjoyed myself thoroughly.

When I went to bed that night there was a glow inside me, deep down. I had found Christmas by giving it away.

A Special Favor

SARA WATSON

December 1971

As the wife of a successful businessman, I had led a carefree and sheltered life. But a sudden setback in his affairs meant I would have to get a job. I took work in a school cafeteria. I bitterly resented the menial job, which included cleaning the big, ugly, and outmoded stove.

The two women with whom I worked elbow to elbow were happy and friendly. Laura talked with just about everyone. When a sobbing first-grader appeared, Laura threw up her hands in mock dismay: "Forgot your lunch for the field trip!" Then she added softly, "I'll fix you one. Come back in ten minutes."

Next it was a teacher. "I'm having six to dinner; what can I serve?" Laura had an answer, "Crab cioppino is easy, good—and expensive. I'll give you the recipe."

Less flamboyant but equally resourceful, Jean often saved the day, or rather the lunch. When the supervisor phoned that because of a strike, bread wouldn't be delivered, Jean volunteered: "My work is almost done, so I'll make four pans of corn bread."

I began to admire Jean and Laura. With four school-age children each—in addition to the job—they rarely complained and never missed the humor of a situation.

However, I found nothing funny about keeping the big black iron-topped gas range clean—especially during the busy week before Christmas, the very time when the public health officer inspected the kitchen. After complaining to all, I announced my intention to clean the stove early the next morning.

The following day I entered the kitchen to begin the grimy job. My eyes jerked to an abrupt focus. A wide red ribbon, tied with a huge bow, encircled a bright, clean stove. The attached card said, "Merry Christmas from Jean and Laura."

What a perfect gift it was, not only of time but of truth—for it told me that the secret of joy in any work is putting people first.

Love Knots

Patricia E. Carr
December 1972

*I*t all began one snowy Saturday, a few weeks before Christmas, when my husband marched into the kitchen. "Mrs. Carr," he said, "I'm going to be working on something in the den that's top-secret. That means you have to promise to keep out."

Since it was the time of year when Santa would be watching, I kept my promise, but the suspense was awful. But while my lips were saying "all right," my mind had already shifted into wondering gear—*What could he be up to?*

After one of his particularly long sessions in the den, I picked up my first clue. The wastepaper basket he emptied into the kitchen trash contained slivers and scraps of multicolored wrapping paper. Why would he be cutting up wrapping paper?

I began to guess: *What if he's making one of those horrible collages he likes so much? He'll probably expect me to hang the darn thing in the living room.* Or, *Maybe it's a mobile. . . . No, he'd never have the patience to balance it. . . .*

My curiosity was at an all-time high when Christmas Eve finally arrived. Santa had left a shoebox for me, taped on all sides. Inside this box was a glass apothecary jar, filled with hundreds of colorful little strips of wrapping paper about the size of those in fortune cookies. Each of these tiny pieces of paper had been tied in a gentle knot. The jar was labeled by my husband's hand:

DR. CARR'S FAMOUS LOVE KNOTS
Taken as directed, Dr. Carr's Love Knots relieve depression, foster well-being, cause good humors to flow and love to grow. Double your love back if satisfied.

"You get to pick one a day," my husband said eagerly, "and you can redeem them anytime you want to."

Carefully untying a red love knot, I read its message aloud, "Good for ten kisses," and turned it in to "Doctor Carr."

Doctor Carr's Love Knots have stretched Christmas into a year-round holiday. "Good for one dish-drying," came to the rescue one Saturday night after we said a late good night to the last of our dinner guests. "Good for a walk," "Turn in for a trip to an antique shop of your choice." But, of all the love knots I have picked, my favorite was three words long. It said, "I love you."

Kitty's Crown

KATHRYN SLATTERY

December 1990

ookies are baking, apple cider is bubbling, four-year-old Brinck and seven-year-old Katy are breathlessly comparing their lists of what they want for Christmas, and I'm getting a little frantic. It's six-thirty P.M., Friday, December 23. From now on it's going to be nonstop cooking and shopping and entertaining. The Christmas tree is shedding like a cat, everything needs cleaning, I haven't wrapped a single gift. . . .

I reach for a package of paper plates and yank the plastic bag open with my teeth. There's a sharp pain at the front of my mouth, and a strange sensation of something giving way. An object clatters on the tile floor. An earring perhaps? But even before my fingers fly up to touch my ears, I grasp the dreadful truth.

"My tooth!" I wail. "My tooth fell out!"

My tongue probes at the empty space where my front tooth should be. Where it is, I discover by getting down on my hands and knees, is beneath the oven. I retrieve the tooth—it's a crown, actually—and as I turn it slowly in my hand, my heart sinks. There, embedded in cement, is the broken-off stub of my real tooth, which for the past twelve years has held the crown in place.

I run to the dining room mirror. All that remains of my tooth is a jagged nib at the gum line.

This can't be happening! Tomorrow is Christmas Eve. The church pageant is this afternoon, and family and friends will be here for Christmas Eve supper. How can I face everyone with a missing front tooth?

I call my dentist, Madeline Apfel. *Oh, Maddy*, I pray, *please be there.* But all I get is her answering machine.

I call our children's dentist. I call my sister's dentist. I call dentists listed in the yellow pages. I even call a dentist in New Jersey.

At the start of the messages I leave, my voice is controlled and brave. But before my message is over I've dissolved into incoherent blubbering. Not helping matters is the fact that a newly acquired lisp has made my name almost impossible to pronounce.

"Thlattery!" I hear myself saying. "Thpelled with an eth, as in 'Thylvethter Cat.'"

As a last resort, I call New York City's Emergency Dental Service hot line. But on Friday night of a holiday weekend, no one is available to help.

"I'm sorry," a weary voice says. "You'll have to call back Monday morning."

My only hope, I'm told, might be found at one of two hospitals in the city which have an emergency-room dentist on call. My husband, Tom, stays home with the kids, and I ask my sister Laurrie to go with me to Beth Israel Hospital.

When we get there, the resident dentist confirms my worst fears: Although he's got emergency-room equipment to wire my jaws shut if I'd been in an accident, he can't help with "routine" work that has to be done by my own dentist. "It could be worse," he says, trying to cheer me up. "The only thing that's hurt is your vanity."

"It's not just my vanity," I wail to my sister as we trudge home. "A part of me is missing. It's as though I've suddenly gone bald or found myself naked in a crowd. I don't want to be laughed at, and I don't want to be lectured. I want thympathy!"

But sympathy is hard to come by—even from my husband. "Aw, c'mon, Kitty," Tom says as I come in the front door with the bad news. "It's just a tooth." Easy for him to say—a man who's never had a cavity in his life.

That night I sleep fitfully and wake exhausted. As the morning drags on, I grow more gloomy and self-absorbed. The Christmas pageant is just hours away. What a sorry soul I must be to allow a silly missing tooth to put a damper on one of the happiest nights of the year.

It's nearly noon when the telephone rings.

"This is Maddy," the woman says, "I just checked my answering machine and got your message from last night. Do you still need help?"

Maddy! Maddy Apfel, my dentist!

"I can see you at two-thirty," she says. "We'll see what we can do."

Maddy's office is a five-minute walk away, and as I head toward Fifth Avenue, I think about the woman waiting for me.

Maddy is unmarried, a striking woman with wide-set eyes and a luxurious mane of blond-streaked hair. And as far as I know, she's the only dentist in New York City who cares enough to drop everything to help a patient in need on Christmas Eve. Just the same, I apologize for inconveniencing her.

"You know, Kitty," she says, clipping a paper bib around my neck, "I've got tons to do. I have company coming for dinner, my apartment's a mess, my tablecloth needs ironing, I haven't wrapped a single gift, and I was beginning to panic. But you know what? It doesn't matter. Your call has helped me to put everything into perspective."

Maddy grins. "In a funny way," she says, "just knowing you need my help is the best Christmas present anyone could give me."

As I lean back and open my mouth, I mull over Maddy's words. *My need . . . a gift? But then, why not?* If Maddy gains satisfaction from helping me, my need was indeed a gift. I begin to relax for the first time in days; in fact, I'm almost glad my tooth fell out. In a way, this whole episode has now helped two frantic women put things into perspective.

For the next ninety minutes Maddy hums along merrily to Christmas carols on the radio as she reinstalls the crown. She says I'll have to return again for more work, but at least I'll have a front tooth to get me through the holidays.

At precisely four o'clock I slip into the church pew between Tom and Brinck. "Everything okay?" whispers Tom.

My smile is all the answer he needs.

The Unopened Gift

December 1992

*I*t was such an unusual thing for T.J. to say.

We were walking in the snow outside our house that cold November afternoon when I reached down, hugged my five-year-old son and told him how much I loved him. Terry Junior looked up through his beautiful green-blue eyes and said, "I love you too, Mommy, more than anything in the world—except God. I love him a little bit more!"

I laughed and tousled his sandy hair. "Well," I said, "as long as it's God, that's okay."

Where in the world had he heard about God? I wondered. God was never mentioned in our house. I had not thought much about God for years, and my husband, Terry, was practically an atheist. Neither of us felt we had need of anything spiritual in our lives. Young and successful, we were doing quite well on our own. We lived in Denver, where Terry was a corporate executive, and I was busy raising our two children.

But T.J.'s declaration of love wasn't the only strange thing that happened in those days. For a week he had been trying to give me his Christmas gift, which he had bought at a PTA-sponsored "Secret Santa Shop." Each time he offered me the little box, wrapped in colored paper, I would laugh. "Honey, it's too early! Please put it away." Finally I took it and said we'd keep it safe in my closet until Christmas.

That night I told Terry about the unopened gift, and I mentioned T.J.'s words about God. Could they have had something to do with the death of Terry's mother six months ago? I asked. Both T.J. and his eight-year-old sister, Samantha, had wondered where she had gone. To soothe them I had said, "With God, in heaven."

Terry nodded thoughtfully.

"And remember," I continued, "not long after that, you and I were talking at the dinner table in front of the children about the man in your office—the one who keeps talking to you about God and Jesus?"

"Yes," he said, "Don, who always asks me to think about where I'll spend eternity. He just doesn't give up."

But we were never to know for sure what caused T.J. to speak as he did. In fact, that night my talk with Terry flared into an argument about other matters. Truth was, our marriage was in trouble. We had grown apart through the years. Now we often found fault, bickered, and snapped at each other. If it hadn't been for Samantha and T.J., we would have parted long ago.

The children remained my greatest solace. I especially doted on T.J. Only recently I had told a friend just how I felt about him. "If anything ever happens to that little guy," I said, "you can lock me up and throw away the key, because I don't know how I would get through it."

I found out that terrible, gray December 3, 1983.

My parents had come for a holiday visit, and we all had gone to a stable on the outskirts of Denver, where Samantha was learning to ride. We planned to take pictures of the children astride a horse for our family Christmas card. It was so cold that Samantha rode her horse inside, up and down the shed row between the stalls. As usual, T.J. ran about making friends with everyone from stable workers to visitors. When Samantha was through with her lesson, I said, "Go get your brother so we can take the Christmas picture."

She came back in a few minutes: "I can't find T.J. anywhere." A chill clutched me. Terry hurried away to look, and I ran to my parents. They hadn't seen T.J. either. I thought of the frozen creek that meandered near the stables. Outside, scanning the flat snow-covered land, I could see no one. I called for T.J., but there was only eerie silence. Meanwhile my parents and Terry questioned everyone in the area, even canvassing homes that bordered the stable property. My calls had turned to screams, and I was stumbling through the snow when Terry came up and took my arm.

"We've looked everywhere," he said huskily. "I'm calling the police."

I fell to my knees in the snow, crying, pleading. "Oh, God, I'll go to church every week, I'll put our children in Sunday school," I bargained. "I'll do anything if you'll please bring my baby back!"

Terry led me with Samantha to a nearby house, where a woman gave me a tranquilizer. I huddled under a quilt, rocking back and forth, crying for my little boy. Hours passed. At around two in the afternoon the people who were trying to comfort me suddenly became quiet. I looked up and saw Terry's grief-stricken face. He knelt and put his arm around me.

"They found him," he said quietly. I didn't want to hear the details of how T.J. had wandered onto a snow-covered pond and had fallen through the ice. "The doctors said he didn't suffer, Anne," said Terry. "The water was so cold he lost consciousness instantly."

The room seemed to fade away for a moment. I remember Terry telling me they were taking T.J. to the hospital, where doctors thought there was a one-in-a-million chance to revive him. More hours seemed to pass as I waited for word. Then there was a call from the hospital: A heartbeat had been found. Hope glimmered. I sat up and, dabbing tear stains from my face, got out my makeup. "T.J. always told me I was beautiful," I said. "I don't want him to see me like this." But there was to be one more call from the hospital. Terry came over and said, "He's gone."

When we walked into our house, now so deadly quiet, the terrible impact of losing T.J. hit me even worse than before. I stood transfixed in the hallway. I wanted to scream, but I couldn't. I stared blindly, my chest convulsing with short gasps. Terry raced upstairs and closed the door to T.J.'s room. I felt myself reeling on the edge of madness.

That's when a picture flashed before me: the gift T.J. had tried to give me so often. I dashed upstairs to our room and reached up to the closet shelf. My fingers touched the package. Pulling it down, I quickly tore away the paper. There in my hand lay a little gold-colored cross on a chain.

As it wavered in my blurred vision and my hand closed tightly on it, I knew with definite certainty where T.J. was—with Jesus Christ in heaven. T.J.'s little cross had broken through that hard, icy wall surrounding me, and I felt myself standing in his presence.

The serenity which flooded into me at that moment must have been visible. Terry stepped over and asked me if I was all right.

I took his hand. "I'm OK, Terry," I whispered. When I showed him T.J.'s gift, he hugged me in silence and wept.

After the funeral, Terry and I did not speak of T.J. We were so numbed, so preoccupied with our own feelings that we barely spoke at all. The snarling and bickering had stopped, but we seemed to live completely separate lives.

One day I looked up addresses of several Christian bookstores. I drove to all of them, and in each one I searched for books that would tell me more about Jesus and heaven. It was as when your child goes off on a trip to another country and you want to find out everything you can about that place. I found myself desperately wanting to know how to get there myself.

The next surprise came a month later. The front bell rang, and when I opened the door a middle-aged, casually dressed stranger smiled at me. "Hello," he said, "I'm Terry's pastor."

I stepped back in complete shock. Terry was away, but I invited Rev. Luther Larson into our living room and listened in amazement as he said how pleased he was to have a new member of his congregation. Then we talked about T.J. He spoke of a couple at his church who had lost a baby daughter to meningitis.

"You could help one another," he said. As he left, he added that he hoped to see me at his service.

That night, the separate paths Terry and I had been traveling came together. During a long talk, Terry told me his story. "Remember Don—the man who kept trying to talk to me about God?" he said. "Well, on that terrible afternoon while T.J. was in the hospital, I called Don for prayer. He put me in touch with Pastor Larson, and I've gone to his church several times since then." He looked up. "Would you ever think of going with me?"

My voice caught. "Oh, Terry," I cried, "yes!" And I told him of my journeys to the bookstores.

Terry and I went to that church and met the parents who had lost their baby. Our visits led to a deep friendship. This was the first of many encounters with bereaved mothers and fathers, who have become our special mission. We believe that any solace we have offered in their time of sorrow is still another part of the gift T.J. gave us.

Gift of the Heart

Norman Vincent Peale

December 1995

New York City, where I live, is impressive at any time, but as Christmas approaches it's overwhelming. Store windows blaze with lights and color, furs and jewels. Golden angels, forty feet tall, hover over Fifth Avenue. Wealth, power, opulence . . . nothing in the world can match this fabulous display.

Through the gleaming canyons, people hurry to find last-minute gifts. Money seems to be no problem. If there's a problem, it's that the recipients so often have everything they need or want that it's hard to find anything suitable, anything that will really say, "I love you."

Last December, as Christ's birthday drew near, a stranger was faced with just that problem. She had come from Switzerland to live in an American home and perfect her English. In return, she was willing to act as secretary, mind the grandchildren, do anything that was asked. She was just a teen. Her name was Ursula.

One of the tasks Ursula's employers gave her was to keep

track of Christmas presents as they arrived. There were many, and all would require acknowledgment. Ursula kept a faithful record, but with growing concern. She was grateful to her American friends; she wanted to show her gratitude by giving them a Christmas present. But nothing that she could buy with her small allowance could compare with the gifts she was recording daily. Besides, even without these gifts, it seemed to her that her employers already had everything.

At night from her window, Ursula could see the snowy expanse of Central Park and beyond it the jagged skyline of the city. Far below, taxis hooted and the traffic lights winked red and green. It was so different from the silent majesty of the Alps that at times she had to blink back tears of homesickness. It was in the solitude of her little room, a few days before Christmas, that an idea came to Ursula.

It's true, she thought, *that many people in this city have much more than I do. But surely there are many others who have far less.*

Ursula thought long and hard. Finally, on her day off, which was Christmas Eve, she went to a large department store. She moved slowly along the crowded aisles, selecting and rejecting things. At last she bought something and had it wrapped in gaily colored paper. She went out into the gray twilight and looked helplessly around. Finally she went up to a doorman, resplendent in blue and gold. "Excuse, please," she said in her hesitant English, "can you tell me where to find a poor street?"

"A poor street, miss?" said the puzzled man.

"Yes, a very poor street. The poorest in the city."

The doorman looked doubtful.

"Well, you might try Harlem. Or down in the Village. Or the Lower East Side, maybe."

But these names meant nothing to Ursula. She thanked the doorman and walked along, threading her way through the stream of shoppers until she came to a policeman. "Please," she said, "can you direct me to a very poor street in . . . Harlem?"

The policeman looked at her sharply and shook his head. "Harlem's no place for you, miss." And he blew his whistle and sent the traffic swirling past.

Holding her package carefully, Ursula walked on, head bowed against the sharp wind. If a street looked poorer than the one she was on, she took it. But none seem like the slums she had heard about. Once she stopped a woman, asking, "Please, where do the very poor people live?" But the woman gave her a stare and hurried on.

Darkness came sifting from the sky. Ursula was cold, discouraged, and afraid of becoming lost. She came to an intersection and stood forlornly on the corner. What she was trying to do suddenly seemed foolish, impulsive, absurd. Then, above the traffic's roar, she heard the cheerful tinkle of a bell. On the corner opposite, a Salvation Army man was making his traditional Christmas appeal.

At once, Ursula felt better; the Salvation Army was a part of life in Switzerland too. Surely this man could tell her what she wanted to know. She waited for the light to change, then crossed over to him. "Can you help me? I'm looking for a baby. I have here a present for the poorest baby I can find." And she held up the package with green ribbon and the gaily colored paper.

Dressed in gloves and an overcoat a size too big for him, he seemed an ordinary man. But his eyes were kind. He looked at Ursula and stopped ringing his bell. "What sort of present?" he asked.

"A dress. For a small, poor baby. Do you know of one?"

"Oh, yes," he said. "Of more than one, I'm afraid."

"Is it far away? I could take a taxi, maybe?"

The Salvation Army man wrinkled his forehead. Finally he said, "It's almost six o'clock. My relief will show up then. If you want to wait, and if you can afford a dollar taxi ride, I'll take you to a family who needs just about everything."

"And they have a small baby?"

"A very small baby."

"Then," said Ursula joyfully, "I will wait!"

The substitute bell-ringer came. A cruising taxi slowed. In its welcome warmth, Ursula told her new friend about herself, how she came to be in New York, what she was trying to do. He listened in silence, and the taxi driver listened too. When they reached their destination, the driver said, "Take your time, miss. I'll wait for you."

On the sidewalk Ursula stared up at the forbidding tenement, dark, decaying, saturated with hopelessness. A gust of iron-cold wind stirred the refuse in the street and rattled the ash cans. "They live on the third floor," the Salvation Army man said. "Shall we go up?"

But Ursula shook her head. "They would try to thank me, and this is not from me." She pressed the package into his hand. "Take it up for me, please. Say it's from . . . from someone who has everything."

The taxi bore her swiftly back from dark streets to lit ones, from misery to abundance. She tried to visualize the Salvation Army man climbing the stairs, the knock, the explanation, the package being opened, the dress on the baby. It was hard to do.

Arriving at the apartment house on Fifth Avenue where she lived, she fumbled in her purse. But the driver flicked the flag up. "No charge, miss."

"No charge?" echoed Ursula, bewildered.

"Don't worry," the driver said. "I've been paid." He smiled at her and drove away.

Ursula was up early the next day. She set the table with special care. By the time she had finished, the family was awake, and there was all the excitement and laughter of Christmas morning. Soon the living room was a sea of discarded wrappings. Ursula thanked everyone for the presents she received. Finally, when there was a lull, she began to explain hesitatingly why there seemed to be none from her. She told about going to the department store. She told about the Salvation Army man. She told about the taxi driver. When she finished, there was a long silence. No one seemed to trust himself to speak. "So you see," said Ursula, "I try to do a kindness in your name. And this is my Christmas present to you. . . ."

How do I happen to know all this? I know it because ours was the home where Ursula lived. Ours was the Christmas she shared. We were like many Americans, so richly blessed that to this child from across the sea there seemed to be nothing she could add to the material things we already had. So she offered something of greater value: a gift of the heart, an act of kindness carried out in our name.

Strange, isn't it? A shy Swiss girl, alone in a great impersonal city. You would think that nothing she could do would affect anyone. And yet, by trying to give away love, she brought the true spirit of Christmas into our lives, the spirit of selfless giving. That was Ursula's secret—and she shared it with us all.

His Mysterious Ways

EVERY CHRISTMAS, I make gifts for family and friends. One year I found an especially beautiful pattern for poinsettia napkin rings. I cut the red and green felt and fashioned it into flowers. Then I grouped them into sets of four and began wrapping. *These are the best gifts I've ever made*, I decided. I checked my list one last time and found I had made one set too many. *I'll keep the last for myself.*

On Christmas Eve I set the dinner table and admired how the napkin rings made everything look perfect. Suddenly my friend Alice came to mind. How could I have forgotten Alice? We always exchanged gifts, and she too made her gifts by hand.

I knew what I had to do: Give Alice my last set of napkin rings. I took the napkins out of the rings and, crestfallen, wrapped them. My table no longer looked so festive.

I called Alice to tell her I was coming over. "I have to run out," she said. "I'll leave your gift in the mailbox."

When my girls and I arrived, we saw the package. I took it out and put her present in its place. "Open it! Open it!" my daughters squealed. Finally I told the girls they could open the present.

"Look, they're napkin rings," Terri said. "Poinsettias. Exactly like the ones you made, Mom."

I could have laughed out loud. *What an amazing coincidence!* I thought. But then a reminder from the book of Luke corrected me: "Give, and it will be given to you" (Luke 6:38, NIV).

—JEAN PADGETT, *December 1997*

"Christmas Don't
Never Come Here"

BILL FLANNAGAN

December 1996

*T*he call had come in early December 1958 from the regional director of home missions for the Presbyterian Church. He had asked me if I would preach for two weekends to a group of people in the coal-mining area near Castlewood, Virginia. A student preacher on my Christmas holiday, I leapt at the chance.

That first Sunday, as I turned off the main highway onto a winding gravel road, I felt as though I had driven into a time warp. Clapboard and tarpaper shacks slumped against the hillside. Smoke eased up over each building in columns like gravestones, and soft oil lamps shone in the windows. But there was not a sound in the early morning gloom, not even dogs barking to announce a stranger was passing. Just black, cold silence.

The church was a simple cement-block building. It had a flat tarpaper roof with a stovepipe for a steeple. The surrounding shacks were unpainted, the ground was barren, everything was covered with soot, and the smell of coal hung in the air.

As the congregation filed in, I noticed their clothing was worn but neat. Their faces were pale and their eyes sunken. Inside, we all gave thanks to God. But there was no indication that this was the Christmas season. No trees, no lights, no wreaths, no red bows.

After the service a woman in a denim jacket introduced herself and her three children, John, Luke, and Sarah. Her name was Mrs. Spense, and she invited me to lunch. A solemn, thoughtful woman, probably in her thirties, although she looked much older, she hurried home to prepare the meal while the three youngsters and I ambled along behind her on the icy path.

We entered a two-room shack by a front door that was so flimsy I could see through it. The main room was illuminated by three kerosene lamps and a potbellied stove glowing like a jack-o'-lantern. Mr. Spense sat in a wooden rocker next to the stove, chewing a pipe with a chipped bowl and broken stem. "Welcome, Preacher," he said. I glanced around the room. The thin, cracked walls were covered with newspaper and torn paper bags to keep out the wind. A tattered quilt hung on a wire to hide the two beds and the cooking area. There was running water, but the outhouse in back was the only bathroom.

The children stood quietly at first. My gaze fell on an old bluetick hound stretched out so close to the stove that I thought I could smell his fur being singed. Snuggled up to his stomach was a raccoon. "Them's Blue and Bandit," John explained. "And them's ours."

We sat for a while, not saying much. Lean and lanky, John

was intent on whittling the bark off a stick with a broken barlow knife, neatly throwing the scraps into the stove fire. Luke took out a river rock and began polishing it intently with a piece of wool. Like a master craftsman, he held it up to the light and blew the dust off, then resumed polishing. Sarah sat by, watching with wide eyes.

Lunch was soon ready. My pie-pan plate had been heaped with potatoes and beans provided by two neighbor ladies. The meat was something Mr. Spense had caught earlier in the week (I didn't ask what). Mrs. Spense said, "Preacher, would you pray for us?" We held hands over a table made of rough planks covered with oilcloth.

I didn't linger after lunch. Excusing myself, I thanked the Spenses for their hospitality. As I stood at the door, putting on my overcoat and gloves, the children eyed me curiously. John reached out and patted the cuffed fur lining of my gloves. I asked Luke about the man's felt hat he wore. He had picked it up along the road. "He don't never take it off," Sarah said. "Even when he sleeps."

I promised to be back the next week, the Sunday before Christmas. Then I asked the children, "What would you like for Christmas?"

"Mr. Preacher," John said, "Christmas don't never come here."

Mrs. Spense put her hand on his shoulder. "Now, John," she said, "there's more important things."

I stepped off the porch, fighting tears. As I drove down the mountain, I was determined that somehow I would bring Christmas to the Spense family.

All week I kept wondering what I could do for them. They were proud people; I couldn't give them a handout. Although the children had no toys, it was clear they entertained themselves easily. They were polite with one another and treated their parents with respect. Their mother's words rang with new meaning: "There's more important things."

The next Sunday, following the morning worship service, I stopped by to drop off some packages for the Spenses. I explained that in my family when people do something kind for us, we have the blessing of sharing some of our resources. It's the giving that's important.

The first present I gave them was a two-foot Christmas tree that had sat on the counter of the corner drugstore back home. The store owner heard me talking with some friends about the plight of people in that coal-dusted place. "Flannagan," he shouted, "how about moving that tree out for me? Maybe someone could use it." Decorated with tinsel and gold ornaments, it sparkled in the Spenses' home.

Next, Mr. Spense unwrapped his pipe. One of my professors, after asking about my weekend, had picked a beautiful pipe from his collection and handed it to me, saying, "Bill, I need to make room for another pipe. Could you pitch this one for me?"

"It's already broke in," Mr. Spense noted as he turned it over in his hands.

I witnessed the first smile I had ever seen on Mrs. Spense's face when she opened a box that held a beautiful wool sweater. My mother had insisted I take it, saying, "Mrs. Spense needs this more than I do."

When John opened his present and found my old Boy Scout pocketknife, his comment was, "Wow!"

Luke paced like old Blue until he could open his gift—the biggest box of all. He tore through the paper and let out a shout when he found one of my dad's gray felt hats. "Perfect fit," he announced, pulling it down over his ears.

Then came Sarah, who had waited patiently for her turn. After opening the wrappings, she exclaimed, "Mama, it's a real baby doll! My first baby doll!"

I had a huge box of food that had been sent by the grocer back home. Mrs. Spense immediately divided up the groceries for the neighbors who had helped supply my feast. Plus, she put aside a few items for some needy families down the hill.

I had not forgotten Blue or Bandit. Blue took his ham bone and worked on it by the stove. As Bandit began to clean his treats, I asked the Spense family if I could pray for them. But before I did, the children spoke up. "Mr. Preacher," said John, "we'uns want to give you something." He proudly gave me the latest stick he had stripped and sharpened. Luke handed me his precious polished river rock. And when sweet Sarah gave me her biggest hug, I wondered, after all, who had brought Christmas to whom?

My Amazing Sheepskin Dream Coat

JOE GARAGIOLA

December 1999

*Y*ou could always tell when Christmas was coming on The Hill, the Italian-immigrant neighborhood in St. Louis where I grew up. The Nativity scene appeared on the lawn of the rectory at St. Ambrose, our church; and the other sure sign was the store windows. They looked a little fancier, with sprayed-on "snow" and the best items on display. It was there, in one of those windows the year I was ten, that I saw the greatest thing I'd ever laid eyes on.

A golden-brown sheepskin coat appeared in the window of Russo's Dry Goods. I'd take the long way home from school just to look at it and daydream about how it would feel buttoned around me. I wanted that coat more than anything, but I knew there was no way in the world I was ever going to get it.

Like most of the men in the neighborhood, my father worked a long, tough day at Laclede-Christy, a clay-pipe factory.

He stretched his paycheck to support our family and to pay the mortgage on our house. We always had food on the table, clothes to wear—I even had mine modeled for me by my big brother, Mickey, who wore them first—and a little to give to our church every week. But that didn't leave anything for luxuries such as a sheepskin coat.

One Sunday evening in early December, I stood in front of Russo's staring at the coat, taking in every detail as if there were something I might have missed all the other times I'd come to see it. The buttery brown leather. The fleece lining that looked almost golden in the right light. The cuffs, fitted so that on a windy day cold air wouldn't shoot up your arms. I pulled my thin cloth jacket a little higher around my neck. It didn't make me feel any warmer. Just the thought of that sheepskin coat did, though, and so close to Christmas, I couldn't think of anything else.

"You see that coat in Russo's window?" I asked as we sat down to dinner that night.

"That'll keep you warm, I guarantee you," said Uncle Tom, who lived with us. "Sheepskin, right?"

My mother set my favorite dish, risotto, on the table. For once I ignored it. "Yeah," I replied. "The coat looks plenty warm." I sneaked a glance at Pop. He smiled, but didn't say anything as he spooned a big helping of risotto onto my plate.

"Probably costs plenty too," Mickey laughed. "That coat would keep you warm even in a St. Louis winter!" We thought St. Louis was the coldest place on earth because we'd never been anywhere else.

"It'd sure be nice to have a coat like that," I hinted.

"It would be nice. A lot of things would be nice. . . ." my father murmured, his thought trailing off like my hopes.

"Pop's right," I said to Mickey as we climbed into bed that night. "Lots of things would be nice, but I'm never gonna get 'em."

I wanted nice new things like other kids had. Not that any of those kids lived on The Hill. My friends got hand-me-downs too. We used cast-off baseball bats, fixing their cracks with nails. We taped up worn-out baseballs to get a few extra innings out of them. The guys who played catcher—I was one—made shin guards by stuffing old copies of *National Geographic* into our socks. Spikes were out of the question; Pop didn't believe in buying shoes you couldn't wear to church or school.

After wearing Uncle Tom's old shoes and Mickey's outgrown clothes for as long as I could remember, I dreamed of having something that was mine alone, something new. My father always taught me to dream big and never give up, so as Christmas got closer, I kept mentioning the sheepskin coat whenever he was within earshot. But he didn't say a word about it.

"What do you guess Pop is thinking?" I asked Mickey one night.

"What's he gonna say?" my brother answered impatiently. "If he told you, 'Forget about that sheepskin coat,' you'd be disappointed for weeks. If he doesn't say anything now, when you don't get it Christmas morning, you'll be disappointed for only a day."

I knew as well as Mickey did that our parents looked at Christmas as a holy day to honor our Lord's birth, not to give presents. We didn't even have a tree. Mickey and I would pull a kitchen chair beside our bed each Christmas Eve, and we'd wake

THE JOY OF GIVING

up the next morning to find an orange on the seat, and maybe a shirt to wear to church. Our big holiday treat was panettone, an Italian fruitcake we ate only once a year.

With no word from Pop, I decided that if I was going to get my sheepskin coat, I'd have to ask somebody else: God. A few days before Christmas, I woke up before my brother and knelt by our bed. *I know I haven't been too good this year, God. But I promise, if you get me that coat, I'll do my best from now on.*

Christmas Eve night, Mickey and I set the chair beside our bed as usual. I don't remember how much I slept, but I sure remember waking up. I'll never forget waking up that morning.

There, draped over the chair, was my sheepskin coat from Russo's!

I jumped out of bed and got down on my knees. Rubbing my face in the golden fleece lining, I thought, *Thanks, God, you did a great job!* Then I threw the coat on—it felt so soft and warm, even better than I'd dreamed—and ran through the house, whooping and hollering.

Then I saw Pop standing in his bedroom doorway. Fat tears ran down his cheeks. I'd never seen my father cry. Still, I knew instinctively these were tears of happiness, like a safety valve on a full heart had opened; and I couldn't hold back my biggest smile.

I wore that sheepskin coat long past winter, late into spring. Good thing I had baseball to get me through the days until it was cool enough for me to put the coat on again. A couple of years later I finally outgrew it, and my mother passed it on to another kid who lived on The Hill.

There was something I got that Christmas I would never outgrow—something I didn't completely understand until the day I signed a contract at age sixteen to play baseball for the St. Louis Cardinals. I left Sportsman's Park with a five-hundred-dollar check, my signing bonus, in my hand. It was a hot, late-summer afternoon, but I was so excited that it might as well have been that Christmas morning all over again.

I took the Grand Avenue streetcar and headed for Laclede-Christy, where my father and the other men from The Hill were just sitting down with their lunch pails. Before Pop could ask what I was doing there, I pressed the check into his hand. He stared at it, then looked at me. Neither of us said anything. We didn't need to. We both knew that the check would fulfill his dream of paying off the mortgage on our house. Watching Pop wipe his eyes and smile made me feel warm in a way no sheepskin coat ever could. I realized then that the joy of Christmas, and of the whole year through, is in giving as my father did—from the heart.

Blessing of the Animals

PATRICIA SULLIVAN

December 2000

*M*y great-grandmother was born in a rural area of
Ireland. She told me that during the great potato
famine, no matter how poor her parents and their neighbors
were, they always put out "a wee bit for the beasties" on
Christmas Eve. This gift—this blessing—was given to the animals in honor of the role they played in the humble stable in
Bethlehem.

So when we moved from the city to a farm in Wisconsin,
my husband and I and our nine children decided to revive this
family tradition.

At midnight on Christmas Eve, we all troop down to the
barn through deep snow that crunches underfoot, and we bring
our gifts to the animals. We check to see that each animal has
fresh water and clean bedding. Then the children take turns giving the horses and colts apples, carrots, oats, and hay. The pigs
are given extra mash and chopped vegetables. The cats and

kittens, who have been playing around our feet, lap up big bowls of warm, frothy milk before getting little bags of catnip the girls have tied up in bundles for them. Our Irish setters—Erin, Big Red, and old Mike—wait patiently for their treat of meat broth and table scraps over dry dog food.

"You are a good and faithful friend," says our youngest daughter, Patti, to each animal in turn, petting it fondly. "We ask the blessing of the animals, in Jesus' name."

When all the animals are fed and comfortable, we trudge back to our own snug home. The air is cold. The stars are bright. The night is silent. It is then that the holiness of Bethlehem's stable becomes very real to me. Our family sleeps then, I think, in heavenly peace.

The Giving Spirit

BRENDA LEE

December 2003

*I*t's our prettiest tree yet! Every ornament on it is a gift from someone who's enjoyed a song of mine, mostly people I've never met. There are manger scenes and Santas, even a tiny jukebox that plays my recording of "Rockin' Around the Christmas Tree." Best of all are the homemade ones—the knitted snowmen and handmade angels that remind me of Christmas when I was a girl.

I've been thinking about my childhood as we fill Christmas baskets this week, my husband and I, our daughters and grand-kids. Canned goods, biscuit mix, a frozen turkey, toys too. It would be simpler to send money to some charity that does this, but I want my grandchildren to know the joy I had as a child. The joy the folks who made these ornaments know. The joy of giving yourself.

When you're poor, I tell the kids, you learn a lot about giving. And I grew up even poorer than most of the folks who will get these baskets.

"Of course," I say as we squeeze in an extra bag of stuffing mix, "when I was very young, I didn't know we were poor." Most of the folks in the red clay country of Georgia back in the 1940s got along on little. If we had even less, well . . . till Daddy was killed, things weren't too bad.

He and Mother worked in the cotton mills, moving from town to town. Their whole married life they never owned a home, never had a car, never lived in a house with an indoor toilet or running water or a telephone. Church was where they forgot all that. I was raised on hours-long Sunday worship, Wednesday night prayer meetings, revivals, gospel singing, and an absolute trust in God.

Christmas was when I first learned that if you don't have money for gifts, you can give of yourself. My sister, Linda, three years older than I, taught me and our little brother to cut star shapes from plain paper and color them with crayons and to string popcorn and cranberries into garlands. We couldn't order the beautiful things in the Sears Roebuck catalog, but Linda and I cut out pictures of dolls and necklaces and pretty dresses and made them into ornaments.

Then the whole family tramped out to the woods and chose a tree. Daddy chopped it down, and we dragged it home and hung the garlands and stars and cutouts on it. Christmas morning there was an orange for each of us. It was the only time all year we had fruit, and I make sure to put oranges in our Christmas baskets now. There was something new to wear from Granny, who made all our clothes, and a homemade toy from Daddy.

One year I asked for something he couldn't make, a bicycle,

like some of the kids at school had. They also had homes with refrigerators and beds all their own, but those things didn't interest me. To speed over the dirt roads, though! Somehow Daddy got me that bicycle. It was a discarded boy's bike, but Daddy cleaned away the rust and painted it fire-engine red. I rode it for years.

The high point of Christmas was church, and to me the best part of any service was the singing. At age four, I began singing solos on Sunday. On Christmas I'd stand before the congregation in my new dress from Granny. No girl could have been happier.

Mother and Linda tell me that at age two I could hear a song on our battery-powered radio once and repeat it note for note, word for word. Linda would take me by the hand, and we'd go skipping down the dirt road to our little country store. Someone would pick me up and stand me on the wooden counter beside the big candy jar. I would sing the country songs I'd heard on the radio the night before while Linda gathered the pennies people tossed. Then Linda and I would run home and pile the precious coins on the kitchen table.

It was Linda's idea, when I was six years old, to enter me in the talent contest that was to change our lives.

Our family's fortunes had gone from bad to worse. The cotton mills weren't hiring, so Daddy found work in a stone quarry. Then he broke his arm, and we had to move to a tenant farm. We kids labored in the fields right beside our parents, dragging the heavy cotton sacks beneath the broiling Georgia sun, fingers bleeding on the thorny bolls. When Daddy's arm mended, he got a construction job. We moved to a rented house in town. It had a dirt yard and a single bedroom for the five of us. But we were out of the cotton fields, and Granny made us new dresses so Linda and I could enter Conyers Elementary School.

That's where Linda learned about the competition open to all schoolchildren in the county. There were to be two prizes, one for beauty and one for talent. Only the beauty contest had a cash prize, and that's the one I set my heart on. Granny made me a pink dress with big puffed sleeves, and Mother put my hair up in pin curls. Best of all, the night before the contest I got to be the first one in the washtub. The water had to be hauled from the well and heated on the stove and by my turn it was always lukewarm. With my hot bath and fancy dress and curls, I was sure I was the most glamorous girl on the stage.

The school auditorium was packed. One by one kids stepped into the spotlight and sang or recited or played an instrument. The audience applauded and the performer sat down.

At last it was my turn. To my surprise, when I finished, people were on their feet cheering and stamping and hollering. I didn't know what to make of it. People didn't carry on like that when I sang at church. My family was real proud of me, but since I hadn't won the cash, I felt like I'd let them down. The prize for the talent winner was a box of peppermint sticks, and I've hated peppermint ever since!

There was an additional prize for talent: a guest appearance on a Saturday morning radio show in Atlanta called *Starmakers Revue*.

Mother scraped together the money for the bus trip to the big city. I sang some songs and was invited back. Saturdays became Mother's and my day out. The show didn't pay anything, and bus fare was hard to come by. But since the sponsor was Borden, I got all the ice cream I could eat. I felt like the richest girl in Georgia.

I was eight when my world fell apart. Daddy was working construction. The man on the scaffolding above him dropped his hammer. It struck Daddy on the head. He never regained consciousness.

Mother had to borrow money so we would have decent things to wear to the funeral. We moved in with her sister Irene. Now my family was really poor. Mother was thirty-two years old with three children to support, no job, and no prospects. But she had something better—an unshakable trust in God, a richness of faith.

And God did supply our needs—in a way none of us could have imagined. From the Atlanta radio show came other invitations for me to sing—at dinners and dances and a poultry convention, and even for TV. I became a regular on a show called *TV Ranch*. I'd never been paid for any of my performances, nor did it occur to my parents to ask for anything. Then, shortly after Daddy's death, in God's mysterious timing, I sang at a luncheon and was handed an envelope. Inside was thirty-five dollars— more than most working men in rural Georgia earned in a week.

Oddly enough, it wasn't until I began earning money that I finally realized just how poor our family had been. Yet I also saw how rich we were too—in faith, in love, in happiness.

"Happiness comes from what you give," I tell our grandkids as we carry the Christmas baskets out to the car, "not what you get." And the most precious thing we have to give is ourselves. It's why I've always put all of me into every song I sing. Why I address and sign every Christmas card I send—more than a thousand of them—by hand. Why I'm grateful to have learned in my childhood that Christmas is a time for giving yourself.

God teaches us this same lesson at Christmas, for isn't that what he did too? He gave his only Son, not in a palace but in a stable, surrounded by humble shepherds, eager to see the greatest gift of all.

A Celebration of Faith

Gold, Circumstance, and Mud

REX KNOWLES

December 1961

*I*t was the week before Christmas.

I was baby-sitting our four older children while my wife took the baby for his checkup. (Baby-sitting to me means reading the paper while the kids mess up the house.)

Only that day I wasn't reading. I was fuming. On every page of the paper, as I flicked angrily through it, gifts glittered and reindeer pranced, and I was told that there were only six more days in which to rush out and buy what I couldn't afford and nobody needed. What, I asked myself indignantly, did the glitter and the rush have to do with the birth of Christ?

There was a knock on the door of the study, where I had barricaded myself. Then Nancy's voice said, "Daddy, we have a play to put on. Do you want to see it?"

I didn't. But I had fatherly responsibilities, so I followed her into the living room. Right away I knew it was a Christmas play, for at the foot of the piano stool was a lighted flashlight wrapped in swaddling clothes in a shoebox.

Rex, age six, came in wearing my bathrobe and carrying a mop handle. He sat on the stool and looked at the flashlight. Nancy, ten, had a sheet draped over her head. She stood behind Rex and began, "I'm Mary and this boy is Joseph. Usually in this play Joseph stands up and Mary sits down. But Mary sitting down is taller than Joseph standing up, so we thought it looked better this way."

Enter four-year-old Trudy at a full run. She never has learned to walk. There were pillowcases over her arms. She spread them wide and said only, "I'm an angel."

Then came Anne, age eight. I knew right away that she represented a Wise Man. In the first place, she moved like she was riding a camel (she had on her mother's high heels). And she was bedecked with all the jewelry available. On a pillow she carried three items, undoubtedly gold, frankincense, and myrrh.

She undulated across the room, bowed to the flashlight, to Mary, to Joseph, to the angel, and to me, and then announced, "I am all three Wise Men. I bring precious gifts: gold, circumstance, and mud."

That was all. The play was over. I didn't laugh. I prayed. How near the truth Anne was! We come at Christmas burdened with gold—with the showy gift and the tinselly tree. Under the circumstances of our time and place and custom, we can do no other. And it seems a bit like mud when we think of it.

But I looked at the shining faces of my children, as their audience of one applauded them, and remembered that a child showed us how these things can be transformed. I remembered that this child came into a material world and, in so doing, eternally blessed the material. He accepted the circumstances, imperfect and frustrating, into which he was born, and thereby infused them with the divine. And as for mud—to you and me it may be something to sweep off the rug, but to all children it is something to build with.

Children see so surely through the tinsel and the habits and the earthly to the love which, in them all, strains for expression.

An Old Man Remembers Four Christmases

MICHAEL G. SATTLER

December 1968

--- *1903* ---

I am an old man now, yet I can see myself as a boy of six trying to hurry Christmas. For weeks the packages "hidden" in the hall closet had danced in my mind until—at last—came the Christmas-morning dash into the parlor. This year, this time, to the dismay of my parents, I stood beside the beautiful tree in deep gloom.

"Santa didn't come," I said. I had seen every one of those packages before.

We opened the gifts, emotions in conflict, but later my wonderful dad took me into the sunroom to talk. Gently he described Santa, not in terms of the merry man I knew, but in terms of spirit. Santa Claus, like Christmas, was much more than gifts and tinsel and candy canes, Dad said; and he reminded me that the Christ Child, with his love, his total generosity, was the real reason for Christmas.

"Michael, when on Christmas morning a house is filled with love and generosity—like ours—Santa has paid his visit."

I nodded a nod that has lasted through the years. Santa had come after all.

1917

What was I doing there in France, a twenty-year-old kid, fighting a war on Christmas Eve? I wanted to be home with Dad and Mom and my brothers instead of shivering in a trench.

It annoyed me when Kevin O'Connor, a young soldier with an appallingly thick Irish started to read aloud, "And it came to pass in those days, that there went out a decree from Caesar Augustus. . . ." Luke, the story of the Nativity. I didn't want to hear it. I turned away, grumbling, but Kevin read on. There was Mary, great with child.

The journey. The shepherds. "And the angel said unto them, Fear not: for, behold, I bring you good tidings of great joy. . . ." Somehow the words insisted upon being heard. My buddies were responding too. And now I was affected. "And suddenly there was with the angel a multitude of the heavenly host praising God. . . ." My loneliness and bitterness lifted. I turned away from my own self-pity and joined a multitude of people, everywhere, praising. That story from Luke shattered the miles between me and New Jersey. Its familiarity and bright strength brought all of us closer together—and close to home.

My wife had been dead a month. I was lonely and heartsick, but mostly I worried about the kind of Christmas our three little girls would have.

Yet, on Christmas morning, they opened their presents with unusual enthusiasm and merriment. And when we were all finished, Catherine, the eldest, spoke up. I knew immediately that every word had been memorized.

"We know how much you miss Mama. We have a surprise for you."

They scampered away. Soon a tiny voice from the bedroom warned, "Close your eyes."

When I opened them, I saw before me the three Wise Men.

"We have no gold," said Catherine.

"Or myrrh," said Sandy.

"Or incense," said Lucille.

"And so," they said in unison, opening their arms wide, "we bring you us!"

I bent down and scooped all three of them into my arms.

It made me feel important when my granddaughter wanted to spend Christmas with me in the old house by the lake. I fussed over every ritual. The eggnog was perfect.

Cathy was to come from Newark. A friend named Al had promised to drive her the fifty-odd miles and then go on. All afternoon the snow had been falling, but finally she arrived.

Al tried to drive home, but after a few slippery miles he had to turn back and was forced to spend Christmas Eve with us. "Well," I said, "let's have an eggnog."

After dinner we sat by the fire and talked about Christmases past. Late in the evening I took out the Bible and read aloud the story of the Nativity.

And Al said, "It's odd, Mr. Sattler, but earlier this evening I missed not being home with the folks. But as you read to us, I began to feel close to them—and closer to you too. It's something strangely powerful—the real Christmas—isn't it?"

I nodded, thinking back to France, touched by the repetition of a young man and his first Christmas away from home.

I have seen Christmas with different people, in different places, and at different times. I am an old man now, and I can tell you that Christmas remains the same—internally beautiful, simple, and eternal as Christ.

Firstborn

LINDA CHING SLEDGE

December 1979

Don't worry," my smiling obstetrician told me. "You're just feeling the third trimester blues. By Christmas you'll be a healthy, happy mommy and won't have time to worry about yourself." But a glance in the mirror on the consultation room wall revealed that I was still the blimpiest of them all.

When I stepped into the hall, I knocked over the red and silver "Merry Christmas" sign that stood on a tripod. Outside, the streets of New York's Upper West Side were icy and gray with piles of sooted snow. I clomped in thick winter boots toward the subway, bending against the wind, wishing I could go home and put my swollen feet into a hot tub. But I had an appointment with the English professor who was advising me about my dissertation. She would be waiting for me. *Some Christmas this will be*, I thought glumly. My first baby, and here I was, six thousand miles away from my family in Hawaii. At twenty-eight, I was still in graduate school and all I had to go "home" to was a small, dark two-and-a-half-room apartment in Queens, an unfinished thesis (about Nativity poems in English literature, ironically), a white cat, and a husband who was just as homesick as I.

It wasn't only the discomfort of this last long month that bothered me. I had real doubts about the future. How would I ever finish school with a baby to take care of? Would I have to abandon my dream of a teaching career just when I was so close?

Squeezing between two slim young secretaries in the subway, I rehearsed the excuses I would give my professor for my unfinished thesis. "I can't meet the December 21 due date because I'm having such a difficult pregnancy. I get dizzy spells standing so long in the library stacks." Or, "My doctor says there are complications and he advises total bed rest." No, I looked too massively healthy.

I surfaced from underground and merged into the flow of pedestrian traffic outside the New York Public Library. I crossed wet, slushy 42nd Street and went into the dark hall of the university building.

Her door was open, a bad sign—I was keeping her waiting. I walked into her office thirty-seven minutes late (she had that sharp European intellectual's insistence on incisive thinking and punctuality). Neat shelves of books rose from floor to ceiling. She sat behind her desk, well dressed in a nicely cut suit, while I tried to shrink inside my green home-sewn parachute. I was convinced that I would be the first pregnant student to flunk out of my program. Several books lay open before her; I could see where passages had been marked in her neat, small handwriting. I dropped my notes into a heap on the rug where they looked at me, as if in reproach of my laziness.

"Sorry I'm late," I stammered. "It's just Christmas, you know?" I wasn't sure that she would understand. Could a Jewish person really comprehend the homesickness that Christians feel at Christmastime when they're far from home? Would her exacting professional standards allow for personal doubt and pregnancy paranoia?

Words of lamentation began to pour out of me in a rush—not the careful excuses I had fabricated on the subway, but the awful truth: how I hadn't been able to concentrate on my work during the last three months; how I missed my parents and couldn't bear facing the holidays and the prospect of giving birth without having them around me; how scared I was to be a mother; how grim, cold, and frightening Nativity poems seemed.

I stopped after a while, exhausted. My career, I was sure, was over before it started. I might as well trade in my small library of much-beloved books and my battered typewriter for a diaper-changing table. Throughout my speech, my professor was silent, her intent look changing gradually to a softer one. Finally she spoke, not sternly or severely, but with gentleness.

"Well, my dear, academics can't stand in the way of nature, you know. You can always finish a thesis later. But a baby—that is something very, very special." She continued, her eyes shining. "I remember twenty-four years ago when my daughter was born. I worked until the week she came. I had to—there was no maternity leave in those days for untenured professors. She was five months old when I went back. My career complicated my life and hers, but it enriched us both." She stopped, looked at me, and smiled. "My daughter is the most important work I have ever done."

We talked then like mothers.

When I rose to go, she handed me one of the books on her desk.

"I thought this might be useful for your thesis," she said. "You can return it when you're ready to come back. Don't worry about worrying. I worried, you worry, Jesus' mother worried—hasn't your reading taught you that? After all, Mary was a mother too. All mothers worry. . . . How else should it be when you are opening the door to the universe?"

She hugged me and let me go. Outside on 42nd Street, as busy shoppers jostled me, I glanced at the book in my hand. *Medieval Folk Carols*—it was a subject I had been wrestling unhappily with for the last eight months. The pages fell open to a passage she had carefully marked beforehand. The lyrics leaped before my eyes. It was an ancient English Nativity carol that I had studied in her class and forgotten. But now, it seemed, I understood the words fully:

> A new year, a new year.
> A child has been born
> To save and to keep us
> All who are forlorn,
> So blessed be the time!
> Blessed be the mother,
> The child also
> With *bene-dicamus domino*.
> So blessed be the time!

Plodding happily down slushy 42nd Street, I thought of Mary's Son. And like Mary, I sang.

I worried. I sang.

A Song for Elizabeth

ROBIN KURTZ

December 1979

ecember snow swept across the parking lot of Crescent Manor Convalescent Home. As the youngest nurse on the staff, I sat with the charge nurse at the north-wing station, staring out the double glass doors and waiting for the first wave of evening visitors. At the sound of bedroom slippers flapping against bare heels, I turned to see Elizabeth, one of our patients, striding down the corridor.

"Oh, please," groaned the charge nurse, "not tonight! Not when we're short-handed already!"

Rounding the corner, Elizabeth jerked the sash of the tired chenille robe tighter around her skinny waist. We hadn't combed her hair for a while, and it made a scraggly halo around her wrinkled face.

"Doop doop," she said, nodding quickly and hurrying on. "Doop doop," she said to the man in the day room slumped in front of the TV, a belt holding him in the wheelchair.

The charge nurse turned to me. "Can you get her and settle her down?"

"Shall I go after her or wait till she comes around again?"

"Just wait—I may need you here before she gets back, and she never does any harm. It's just that ridiculous sound she makes. I wonder if she thinks she's saying words!"

A group of visitors swept through the front doors. They came in, scraping their feet on the rug, shaking snow from their coats, cleaning their glasses. They clustered around the desk seeking information; and as they did, Elizabeth came striding by again. "Doop doop," she said happily to everyone. I moved out to intercept the purposeful strider.

"Elizabeth," I said, taking the bony elbow, "I need you to do something for me. Come and sit down and I'll tell you about it." I was stalling for time. This wasn't anything we'd learned in training, but I'd think of something.

The charge nurse stared at me and, shaking her head, turned her attention to the group of visitors surrounding the desk. Nobody ever got Elizabeth to do anything. We counted it a good day if we could keep her from pacing the halls.

Elizabeth stopped. She looked down into my face with a puzzled frown. "Doop doop," she said.

I led her to a writing table in the day room and found a piece of paper and a pencil with a rounded lead.

"Sit down here at the desk, Elizabeth. Write your name for me."

The watery eyes grew cloudy. Deep furrows appeared between her brows. She took the stubby pencil in her gnarled hand and held it over the paper. Again and again she looked down at the paper and up at me questioningly.

"Here. I'll write it first, and then you can copy it, OK?"

In large, clear script, I wrote, "Elizabeth Goode."

"There you are. You stay here and copy that. I'll be right back."

At the edge of the day room I turned, half expecting to see her following me, but she sat quietly over the paper, pencil in hand. The only sound now came from the muffled voices of visitors and their ailing loved ones.

"Elizabeth's writing," I told the charge nurse. I could hardly believe it.

"Fantastic," she said calmly. "You'd better not leave her very long. We don't have time to clean pencil marks off the walls tonight." She turned away, avoiding my eyes. "Oh, I almost forgot. Novak and Sellers both have that rotten flu. They'll be out all week. Looks like you'll be working Christmas Eve." She pulled a metal-backed chart from the file and was suddenly very busy.

I swallowed hard. Until now, I loved my independence, my own little trailer. At twenty-two, I was just out of nurse's training and on my own. But I'd never before spent Christmas Eve away from my parents and my brothers. That hadn't been in the picture at all when I moved away from home. I planned to go home for the holidays.

Words that wouldn't come past the lump in my throat raced through my head: *They'll go to the candlelight service without me! They'll read the stories, and I won't be there to hear! What kind of Christmas can I have in a little trailer with nothing to decorate but a potted fern? How can it be Christmas if I can't be the first one up to turn on the tree lights? Who'll make the cocoa for the family?*

Tears burned my eyes, but I blinked them back. Nodding slowly, I walked toward the day room.

Elizabeth sat at the writing table staring down at the paper in front of her. Softly I touched my hand to the fragile shoulder, and the old woman looked up with a smile. She handed me the paper. Under my big, bold writing was a wobbly signature.

"Elizabeth Goode," it read.

"Doop doop," said Elizabeth with satisfaction.

Later that night, when all the visitors were gone, and the north wing was dark and silent, I sat with the charge nurse completing charts.

"Do you suppose I could take Elizabeth out tomorrow?" I asked. In good weather, we often took the patients for walks or rides, but I didn't know about snowy nights. "I'd like to go to the Christmas Eve service, and I think she'd like to go with me."

"Wouldn't she be a problem? What about the 'Doop doop'?"

"I think I can explain it to her. You know, nobody else talks during church, so she'd probably be quiet too. Look how well she did this afternoon when I gave her something to do."

The charge nurse looked thoughtful. "Things would be a lot easier around here if you did take her. Then you could get her ready for bed when you got back. There'll be visitors to help with the others, but nobody has been here for Elizabeth in a long time. I'll ask her doctor for you."

And so it was that a little first-year nurse and a tall, skinny old lady arrived at First Church on Christmas Eve just before the service began. The snow had stopped, and the stars were brilliant in the clear, cold sky.

"Now, Elizabeth," I said, "I don't know how much you can understand, but listen to me. We're going in to sit down with the rest of the people. There'll be music and someone will read. There'll be kids in costumes too. But we aren't going to say anything. We'll stand up when it's time to sing, and we'll hold the hymnal together."

Elizabeth looked grave. "Doop doop," she said.

Oh, Lord, I hope she understands! I thought. *Suppose she gets up and heads down the aisle wishing everyone a "Doop doop"?*

I wrapped Elizabeth's coat and shawl around her and tucked my arm under hers. Together we entered the candlelit church. Elizabeth's watery old eyes gleamed, and her face crinkled in a smile. But she said nothing.

The choir entered singing. The pastor read from the Bible: "And there were in the same country shepherds . . ."

Costumed children took their places across the front of the church—shepherds and Wise Men, angels and the holy family. Elizabeth watched, but she said nothing. The congregation rose to sing "Joy to the World." Elizabeth stood holding the hymnal with me, her mouth closed. The lights in the sanctuary dimmed, and two white-robed angels lighted the candelabra. Finally, the organ began the introduction to "Silent Night," and we stood up.

I handed the hymnal to Elizabeth, but the old woman shook her head. A cold dread gathered at the back of my neck. *Now what?* Was this the moment when she started down the aisle? I looked at the wrinkled face out of the corner of my eye, trying to guess her thoughts. The singing began. I sang as loudly as I could, hoping to attract Elizabeth's attention. As I paused for breath, I heard a thin, cracked voice.

"Sleep in heavenly peace," it sang. "Sleep in heavenly peace."

Elizabeth! Staring straight ahead, candles reflected in her eyes, she was singing the words without a hymnal.

Oh, Lord, forgive me, I prayed. *Sometimes I forget. Of course it can be Christmas with only a fern to decorate. Of course it can be Christmas without a tree or the family or cocoa. Christmas is the story of love. It's the birth of the Son of God, and it can live in the heart and memory of a gray-haired old woman.*

"Christ the Savior is born," sang Elizabeth. "Christ the Savior is born."

"Merry Christmas, Elizabeth," I whispered, gently patting her arm.

"Doop doop," she said contentedly.

Rome—a Long Way from Home

JOSEPH CALDWELL

December 1983

*J*ust before noon, the bands in different parts of the great piazza were already playing, not necessarily the same tune, but vigorously and very much in the spirit of the day. Most of the enormous throng had already gathered, and there was just enough pushing and shoving to warm us up on a brisk December day in Rome. I was in St. Peter's Square, and in a few moments Pope John Paul II would step out onto the balcony above the portico of the basilica and ask God's blessing on "the city and the world."

This is one of the great events of a true Roman Christmas, and even though I'm a Catholic, it was the "event" that had brought me there more than the wish for a blessing. My thoughts and feelings were elsewhere. I was in the square mostly because that was the place to be.

I am a writer, and for over a year I'd been in Rome under

extremely fortunate circumstances. A novel I'd written had won the *Prix de Rome,* the Rome Prize, which meant a fellowship at the American Academy in Rome. That in turn meant a place to live, a studio where I could write undisturbed, meals, a monthly stipend, opportunities for travel; but now that was about to end. No—more than end, it was about to reverse itself. I'd be returning to absolute uncertainty—no job, no money, no real prospects in sight. I did not want to go.

And there was something else that weighed my spirit down that Christmas morning. This was 1980. On a Sunday night in late November of that year, a powerful earthquake had struck the ancient hill towns above and to the east of Naples. Thousands were killed, hundreds of thousands were homeless, without food or medicine. Rain and snow and cold followed as if to mock the calamity with further hardship.

I'd been to some of these towns the previous October. I had seen these people struggling to work the rock-strewn soil. I had seen the ancient towns, the stones patiently, arduously, raised one on top of another to make a house, a church, a garden wall, a well. These were people who had endured much, and with a dignity that brought an almost serene beauty to their meanest labors.

Now I'd seen these towns, these people, again, on television, in the newspapers. I watched a man struggling among the rubble to retrieve a rake; a woman bending down into a heap of stones to pick up a cooking pot; a stunned family with three children sitting on the remains of a wall, too numb to even weep. It seemed to me that these were people who'd had nothing more than their stones to begin with—and now these very stones had tumbled down around their heads, killing, destroying, undoing the patient work of centuries.

Some of us at the academy wanted to go south, to do what we could to help, but we were told we'd only be more mouths to feed, more people to shelter. So we collected money and clothes, we gave blood. Some of us, I know, prayed. Some of us wept. But there was nothing more we could do except grieve.

Still, it was Christmas and I was in Rome. If I couldn't rejoice, I could at least put myself through the motions. Which is why I'd come to St. Peter's. And now it was noon. The great bell of the basilica was about to toll the hour. The crowd had grown, filling the entire piazza, the tension rising in expectation of the pope's appearance.

I was toward the far end of the square with the full throng in front of me, families with children, tourists, members of religious orders, and regular citizens of Rome. There were banners and placards of the homemade variety; there were photographers and teenagers perched on the base of the Egyptian obelisk that Caligula had brought to Rome. Ranks of police, uniformed in colors more consistent with Christmas than with their calling, were stationed not far from the long incline of steps that led to the massive doors of the basilica itself. The spirit was one of cheerful exhilaration, but I was there more in body than in spirit. My petty concerns about my future and my deeper sorrow for others were all the more keenly felt because of the contrast between the crowd's mood and my own. I was sorry not to be open to the joy all around me, but there didn't seem to be much I could do about it.

Then the huge bell tolled, the doors to the balcony opened, and the Holy Father stepped forward, his hand raised in greeting. The crowd roared a Christmas greeting of its own, waving, holding high the banners and placards with messages to the pontiff. The bands found new strength, strangers turned to each other, shouting, laughing, sharing the moment's joy. I did no more than lift a single hand and wave it with no more enthusiasm than if I were a child again in Wisconsin waving at a passing freight train.

It was then, however, that I noticed, off to my left and a little in front of me, a family grouped around a boy of about eight. He was holding a sign on a pole, waving it with all his might—not an easy task considering the size of the boy and the size of the sign. The family—what seemed to be his parents, grandparents, and younger brother—was cheering not the pope but the boy, urging him to raise the sign higher, to wave it more wildly. To say the least, the boy obliged.

This family was not Roman. Their faces were weather-worn, their clothes were rougher, ill-fitting, of more durable material. Also, by their pride in the boy, in the sign, they seemed to have a solemnity, even as they cheered. How fortunate they were to be so filled with the Christmas spirit. I envied them.

The crowd finally quieted. In the silence, the pope called out the words: "*Cristus natus est!*" or, "Christ is born!" Again the crowd went wild, as if this great good news was being proclaimed for the first time in history, the sudden fulfillment of an old, enduring hope. Again the placards and the banners waved, the boy and his family more exultant than before. In his exuberance, the boy turned every which way, sharing his message with the entire throng.

I saw the sign. It was old and yellowed, the paint lacquered over to preserve it. Around its edges were leaves with birds that looked like chickens and roosters. The lettering was in a semi-script as if the painter had tried to duplicate medieval manuscripts and hadn't quite succeeded. The first letter of each word was gold, the others blue. My impression was that it was a revered family tradition to bring this particular sign to St. Peter's each Christmas. Then I read the words:

> BUON NATALE AL PAPA
>
> LA GENTE DI BAVANO

I knew of Bavano. It was a hill town to the south. It had been all but completely destroyed by the earthquake. These could have been the people I'd seen searching the ruins for a cooking pot or a rake; this could have been the stunned family on the broken wall.

The shouting of the crowd became a distant din; the waving, shoving throng, an indistinct blur, as I found myself joining in and flinging out words, Italian words, words that a few minutes before I had not felt at all like even uttering. "*Buon Natale!*" I heard myself cry. "*Buon Natale . . . buon Natale . . .*" I was waving both arms, and my throat was getting raw. But I kept right on shouting.

These people had risen from their harsh sorrow to proclaim their joy. Nothing, they seemed to say, nothing cancels the coming of Christ; nothing mutes the glad tidings of the angels' song, neither petty concerns nor deepest sorrow. With their shouting and waving they were telling me that Christmas doesn't dismiss unhappiness or undo tragedy; it joins with it. Christ didn't come to end sorrow: he came to become a part of it.

"*Buon Natale!*" I called again—but added now another phrase. "*Buon Natale . . . alla gente di Bavano!*" or, "Merry Christmas . . . to the people of Bavano!"

Of course they couldn't hear me. But Christ could. Which is why, each Christmas since, and probably for all the Christmases of my life, I'll add to the whispered moments of my celebration: "*. . . e buon Natale alla gente di Bavano!*"

The Painter of Light

Thomas Kinkade

December 2000

One afternoon, early in my career, I attended a showing of my work in a small gallery in northern California. Among the people who stopped by to see my paintings, there was a man who wandered in off the street, saw the brightly lit artwork (as well as the complimentary hors d'oeuvres!) and decided to stroll around the show. After making his rounds, he pulled up beside me. "So," he said, "why does this Kinkade guy have all the lights on in his paintings?"

"I couldn't tell you," I confessed.

"Well, if you see him," said the man, "ask him for me."

In a sense, I have spent my career trying to answer that question. When I was a child, I would come home after school and our house would often stand empty, dark, and cold. I'd hope, as I approached, that the lights would come on suddenly—that someone would swing open the door and wave and smile as I quickened my step.

I could hope, but I knew that no one would be home. My father had left us when I was little, so my mother worked late as a secretary to support the family. My brother and sisters frequently got home from school after I did. I would scuff my heels along the sidewalks beside shadowy hedges and sycamore trees. I would stop and study a bird's nest or some wildflowers or perhaps the way wood smoke curled out of chimneys on cool days, but mostly I'd look at all the other houses I passed, the lights on in their windows, the brightness so inviting that I wanted to dash up and ring the bell and wait to be offered some cookies and warm cinnamon milk.

When I finally reached my house, I was hesitant to open the door and go in. It was more than just being afraid of the dark. The lights within other houses on our street filled me with longing. I wished the whole world could be lit up like those houses. Even as a latchkey kid, I was a bit of a romantic.

By no means would I describe my childhood as a miserable one. Nothing could be further from the truth. In the foothills of the California Sierras, in the small town of Placerville, we Kinkade children—I, my older sisters, and younger brother—enjoyed a blessed upbringing. My brother and I made a tree house in our backyard and rolled go-carts down our drive. We attended services at a country church down the lane from our house, the Kinkade clan taking up the length of a pew. I would sit mesmerized not by the voice from the pulpit, but by the blue glass windows overhead and flickering yellow lights of the candles at the altar.

The Placerville of thirty-five years ago was an innocent

place and time, the kind of town where we could ride our bikes to Main Street for a haircut and a bag of dime-store popcorn without our mother worrying, where a boy could deliver the local paper to the door of a pretty girl who would one day become his wife. And it was a place where a boy could have his dream of becoming a painter nourished, his ever-supportive mother framing his drawings on the living room wall, right next to inexpensive prints by his heroes, Norman Rockwell and Rembrandt.

After high school, I took all my romantic aspirations and small-town innocence with me to the University of California at Berkeley. I wanted to become an artist of the people, a communicator with paint, the next Norman Rockwell. I had a desire to touch people's lives with my paintings, and I believed that if I could be true to myself, if I could express my feelings and paint from my heart, my work would speak to people. Why else would I want to paint but to share the joy and light I felt inside with others?

Talk about culture shock! My homespun values were about to clash with twentieth-century intellectualism. No one at Berkeley seemed to find much merit in my idealistic approach. People were creating art around dark or pessimistic themes, exploring tortured inner feelings, childhood pain, and personal insecurities. My fellow students urged me to get in touch with inner demons. My paintings were deemed clichéd and sentimental and outdated.

I suppose I should be grateful for that period of my life, for the way my beliefs were tested. But at the time, each class hour felt like a blow to the stomach, my professors all fighting to tear down my idealism. To them, artwork was supposed to shock and disturb the viewer, not provide comfort and joy. In my dorm room at night, I would lie awake, plagued by doubts. I worried that my professors had it right, that my vision was naive and simplistic. The light began to fade from my dream.

By the end of the year, I gave up on the art program altogether and switched to the College of Liberal Arts, studying literature and humanities. With each spare hour I had, I painted alone in a basement studio and did illustrations for a local newspaper, but every day was a struggle to discover how I could ever become the painter I'd vowed to be.

I'd pray for counsel, but didn't have any answer besides quietly painting and drawing and keeping my creative flame alive through work and hope. Then one day a friend asked me to a revival meeting and, to my surprise, I said yes. I was twenty-two years old and I had not gone to church regularly since I'd left home. I remembered the lights and glass and burning candles of my hometown chapel. Maybe the smell of a church would lift my spirits.

But the auditorium was dark and uninviting, part of an abandoned college, and I wondered what good could come out of a place as dreary as this. With its faded drapes and dusty windows, I couldn't see the slightest promise of light in the place. However, as the enthusiastic young preacher's voice rose and his words, like a long-lost lifeblood, reached my heart, I felt something good within me stir. It was like the feeling I once got looking at a house all ablaze with the warmth of light, as if at last I had found home.

"God's in the room," the preacher was saying. "He's waiting to touch your life, to meet your every need, to fill your life with light. He's here. If you want to know him, come down to the altar. Come down to the altar now."

Without consciously willing it, I was suddenly rising and making my way down the aisle to the preacher, his words entering me like light enters glass. At the front of the auditorium, I found myself kneeling. *Open the doors*, I was praying. *Open the doors you want me to go through, God. I commit whatever talents I have to you. If there is any way you want to use me, please show me the direction clearly, dear God.*

I felt myself filled with what I'd always wanted to fill my canvases with, felt lifted out of the dark morass of confusion. I sensed a freedom I'd never known before, freedom to paint as I had always wanted to. And from that day, it has been my life's mission to fulfill that dream of light and bring it to people.

I finished at Berkeley and went on to the Art Center College of Design in Pasadena, where some of my teachers did encourage my traditional approach. Along the way I seemed to be living out the cliché of the starving artist—working late into each evening and scrimping for art materials and tuition. I tell you, those years were lean, but things were also falling into place for me.

A fellow artist, James Gurney, and I ended up traveling across America after two years at Art Center. We were, as the newspapers called us, two young "hobo artists." In the process of working and traveling, we came up with the idea for a sketcher's handbook and hit New York with a book proposal in hand. *The Artist's Guide to*

Sketching came to life and became an art-instruction success by the time I was twenty-four years old.

In 1982, I married my childhood sweetheart, Nanette, and we returned home to Placerville, not far from where I'd first seen her on my paper route. My paintings soon started to sell. In fact, I couldn't keep up with the demand. To reach more people, Nanette and I experimented with ways my work could be reproduced, including a process in which the print's inked image can be bonded with artist's canvas. With a few touches by trained artisans, the reproduced work on canvas had all of the appearance and texture and warmth of an original oil painting.

To convey hope and joy to others, the scenes I paint are alive with light. Each canvas is infused with brightness, because I believe this is how the world can be and sometimes is. A lighted window says home to me. It says all is well with the world, someone's waiting, someone cares.

Most of all, light exists in the dimension of the spirit. It was what God first created, and it is probably the most consistent metaphor in all of Scripture. Truth is represented as light, and in Matthew 5:16, Christ affirms that each of us should "Let your light so shine before men, that they may see your good works, and glorify your Father which is in heaven." But light is something you can't hold. You can't touch or taste or pin down its subtle, constantly changing effects. As a painter, light is the essence of what I try to capture on canvas—a light that dispels darkness, that chases away confusion and despair.

However, for me, the brightest light burns inwardly. With this supernatural, inspiring light, God illuminates our spiritual path and leads us to heaven through the love of his Son. And heaven, at least in my artistic imagination, is a place where the windows always glow.

His Mysterious Ways

ONE COLD WINTER NIGHT, as my wife, daughter, and I headed home from shopping, I was deep in thought because I had just accepted a job as the director of a boys' home. Now my decision was troubling me. *Did I make the right choice in taking the position?*

I drove carefully because it was not unusual to come across deer on the highway in this part of Indiana. That was it. "Lord," I said aloud, "if you love me, let me see a deer tonight."

"Oh, you know the Lord loves you," my wife said.

"Yes," I replied, "but I need reassurance that I am following his will."

My senses and vision were heightened as I drove. But nothing, not even an old farm cat, appeared. Disheartened, I turned into our gravel driveway and pulled into the garage. Nothing. Not a deer in sight.

While Jackie and Susannah juggled packages into the house, I trudged over to the mailbox. I pulled out a handful of letters and made my way to the front door while idly flipping through the mail. A bill, another bill, a fund-raising letter, two Christmas cards, then a third. I stopped. On the third card, glowing under the porch light, was a stamp, and on the stamp was unmistakably a deer.

In that moment I knew I had made the right decision. I had seen God's deer. I had felt God's love.

—BOB RAWLINS, *December 1996*

Yuletide Miracles

On the Top of the World

JOHN H. BLUE

December 1950

When nineteen years old and just out of school, I packed a sledge one day, in preparation for a trip some five hundred miles north of Dawson, up in the Yukon. This was to be the first Christmas I had ever spent alone, and my most hazardous journey in the dead of winter.

My objective was to chart a ledge that was only partly indicated on a crude map drawn two years previously. The markings on the map were reliable, but I hardly anticipated the variety of hazards ahead.

The trail was over ice and snow, frozen rivers and lakes, and steep grades and rock hills. I knew I could expect blizzards, hungry wildlife, and the peril of food shortage if delayed for any length of time.

I have never started on a trip of this type without talking straight to God, making it clear what my mission is and asking his divine protection for both myself and my dogs. I believe his help can come while I'm "on the run" or when in a church, if the prayer is honest and sincere.

On December 24th, 1908, I was camped about two hundred and fifty miles out of Dawson, in a desolate, moonlit spot, with nothing but snow-covered mountains in the distance and the dogs by my side.

The weather had been fine and the going good, all of which made me deeply grateful. While preparing my Christmas Eve meal of tea and bacon over the pitch stick fire, I thought of my family, thousands of miles away, gathered around the fireplace with Christmas gifts under the tree.

I could see the faces and guess much of the talk that was going on. I also knew that Mother was thinking just as strongly about me and my progress as I was of her and the rest of the family. It seemed as if I could hear her prayer. I straightened up and said, "God, you are being good to me and my dogs. I know you will comfort Mother in her thoughts and let her know that I am all right, and not lonely or cold, even though far away."

I was startled from my thoughts by a hissing sound in the distance. In seconds, the hisses changed to sharp, crackling reports. I looked around quickly as the sounds grew louder. I saw the sky begin to brighten in the north. Multicolored shafts of light shot skyward. The glory of it took my breath away! It was the aurora borealis in full splendor.

There I was with a reserved seat at a private showing of the greatest Christmas pageant one can ever hope to see. All the colors of the rainbow reflected on the snow-covered mountains and flickered over the smooth, snowy surface. It had the effect of a magnificent, shimmering oriental rug.

Just then, the dogs began to growl. They were tense. They stood as still as iron statues. I scanned the horizon. There, coming toward us from the distance, was a pack of wolves. All the beauty was suddenly blacked out in the thought of self-preservation.

I knew my dogs and I were windward from the pack. I hoped the brilliant lights would distract them from seeing us too easily.

But for how long?

To my dismay the wolves formed a large circle about a hundred yards in front of us. I could count fourteen wolves. Then the leader of the pack took his place in the center of that sitting circle and began to howl to the moon. Soon, there was a full chorus of fourteen howling, hardly symphonic voices.

For over an hour this howling kept up as my tension mounted. Then, as the aurora borealis began to sink back into the northern earth, the leader of the pack abruptly stopped his howling, turned, and started back in the direction from which he had come. The others filed behind him.

I was relieved, puzzled, and so in awe that I could hardly believe what I had seen. Had the wolves put on a worship ceremony for my benefit? I haven't heard a church bell ring since that doesn't remind me of this, my most spectacular Christmas experience.

An Exchange of Gifts

DIANE RAYNER

December 1983

I grew up believing that Christmas was a time when strange and wonderful things happened, when wise and royal visitors came riding, when at midnight the barnyard animals talked to one another, and in the light of a fabulous star God came down to us as a little child. Christmas to me has always been a time of enchantment, and never more so than the year that my son Marty was eight.

That was the year that my children and I moved into a cozy trailer home in a forested area just outside of Redmond, Washington. As the holiday approached, our spirits were light, not to be dampened even by the winter rains that swept down Puget Sound to douse our home and make our floors muddy.

Throughout that December, Marty had been the most spirited, and busiest, of us all. He was my youngest—a cheerful boy, blond-haired and playful, with a quaint habit of looking up at you and cocking his head like a puppy when you talked to him.

Actually, the reason for this was that Marty was deaf in his left ear, but it was a condition that he never complained about.

For weeks I'd been watching Marty. I knew that something was going on with him that he was not telling me about. I saw how eagerly he made his bed, took out the trash, and carefully set the table and helped Rick and Pare prepare dinner before I got home from work. I saw how he silently collected his tiny allowance and tucked it away, spending not a cent of it. I had no idea what all this quiet activity was about, but I suspected that somehow it had something to do with Kenny.

Kenny was Marty's friend, and ever since they'd found each other in the springtime, they were seldom apart. If you called to one, you got them both. Their world was in the meadow, a horse pasture broken by a small winding stream, where the boys caught frogs and snakes, where they'd search for arrowheads or hidden treasure, or where they'd spend an afternoon feeding peanuts to the squirrels.

Times were hard for our little family, and we had to do some scrimping to get by. With my job as a meat wrapper and with a lot of ingenuity around the trailer, we managed to have elegance on a shoestring. But not Kenny's family. They were desperately poor, and his mother was struggling to feed and clothe her two children. They were a good, solid family; but Kenny's mom was a proud woman, very proud, and she had strict rules.

How we worked, as we did each year, to make our home festive for the holiday! Ours was a handcrafted Christmas of gifts hidden away and ornaments strung about the place.

Marty and Kenny would sometimes sit still at the table long

enough to help make cornucopias or weave little baskets for the tree; but then, in a flash, one would whisper to the other, and they would be out the door and sliding cautiously under the electric fence into the horse pasture that separated our home from Kenny's.

One night shortly before Christmas, when my hands were deep in peppernöder dough, shaping tiny nutlike Danish cookies heavily spiced with cinnamon, Marty came to me and said in a tone mixed with pleasure and pride, "Mom, I've bought Kenny a Christmas present. Want to see it?" *So that's what he's been up to,* I said to myself. "It's something he's wanted for a long, long time, Mom."

After carefully wiping his hands on a dish towel, he pulled from his pocket a small box. Lifting the lid, I gazed at the pocket compass that my son had been saving all those allowances to buy. A little compass to point an eight-year-old adventurer through the woods.

"It's a lovely gift, Martin," I said, but even as I spoke, a disturbing thought came to mind. I knew how Kenny's mother felt about their poverty. They could barely afford to exchange gifts among themselves, and giving presents to others was out of the question. I was sure that Kenny's proud mother would not permit her son to receive something he could not return in kind.

Gently, carefully, I talked over the problem with Marty. He understood what I was saying.

"I know, Mom, I know . . . but what if it was a secret? What if they never found out who gave it?"

I didn't know how to answer him. I just didn't know.

The day before Christmas was rainy and cold and gray. The three kids and I all but fell over one another as we elbowed our way about our little home putting finishing touches on Christmas secrets and preparing for family and friends who would be dropping by.

Night settled in. The rain continued. I looked out the window over the sink and felt an odd sadness. How mundane the rain seemed for a Christmas Eve. Would wise and royal men come riding on such a night? I doubted it. It seemed to me that strange and wonderful things happened only on clear nights, nights when one could at least see a star in the heavens.

I turned from the window, and as I checked on the ham and lefse bread warming in the oven, I saw Marty slip out the door. He wore his coat over his pajamas, and he clutched a tiny, colorfully wrapped box in his pocket.

Down through the soggy pasture he went, then under the electric fence, across the yard to Kenny's house, and up the steps on tiptoes, shoes squishing. He opened the screen door just a crack and placed the gift on the doorstep. Then he drew a deep breath, reached for the doorbell, and pressed on it hard.

Quickly Marty turned and ran down the steps and across the yard in a wild race to get away unnoticed. Then, suddenly, he banged into the electric fence.

The shock sent him reeling. He lay stunned on the wet ground. His body tingled and he gasped for breath. Then slowly, weakly, confused and frightened, he began the grueling trip back home.

"Marty," we cried as he stumbled through the door, "what happened?" His lower lip quivered, his eyes brimmed.

"I forgot about the fence, and it knocked me down!"

I hugged his muddy little body to me. He was still dazed, and there was a red mark beginning to blister on his face from his mouth to his ear. Quickly I treated the blister; with a warm cup of cocoa soothing him, Marty's bright spirits returned. I tucked him into bed, and just before he fell asleep he looked up at me and said, "Mom. Kenny didn't see me. I'm sure he didn't see me."

That Christmas Eve I went to bed unhappy and puzzled. It seemed such a cruel thing to happen to a little boy while on the purest kind of Christmas mission, doing what the Lord wants us all to do—giving to others, and giving in secret at that. I did not sleep well that night. Somewhere deep inside I think I must have been feeling the disappointment that the night of Christmas had come and it had been just an ordinary, problem-filled night, no mysterious enchantment at all.

But I was wrong.

By morning the rain had stopped and the sun shone. The streak on Marty's face was very red, but I could tell that the burn was not serious. We opened our presents, and soon, not unexpectedly, Kenny was knocking on the door, eager to show Marty his new compass and tell about the mystery of its arrival. It was plain that Kenny didn't suspect Marty at all, and while the two of them talked, Marty just smiled and smiled.

Then I noticed that while the two boys were comparing their Christmases, nodding and gesturing and chattering away, Marty was not cocking his head. When Kenny was talking, Marty seemed to be listening with his deaf ear. Weeks later a report came from the school nurse, verifying what Marty and I already knew: "Marty now has complete hearing in both ears."

The mystery of how Marty regained his hearing remains just that—a mystery. Doctors suspect, of course, that the shock from the electric fence was somehow responsible. Perhaps so. Whatever the reason, I just remain thankful to God for the good exchange of gifts that was made that night.

So you see, strange and wonderful things still happen on the night of our Lord's birth. And one does not have to have a clear night, either, to follow a fabulous star.

Dream Warning

EDWARD CUSHING

December 1993

When I arrive at the scene, the old frame house on Chicago's South Side is burning furiously. Smoke and embers dance crazily in the windy winter night. I give the order to unroll the hoses and then dash madly inside. I pull out three people and administer CPR to two of them before the ambulance arrives, rubber screeching on asphalt. When the blaze is finally under control, someone from the fire department comes up to me. "You did a great job, Captain Cushing," he says, "but two of those three people you pulled out didn't make it."

"No!" I cry. "They're all alive!"

"I'm sorry, Cushing."

Suddenly I awoke in a drenching sweat, my heart racing. My wife, Rosemary, was awake too, staring at me. "Honey, what's wrong?" she asked. "You were shouting."

"Nothing," I mumbled, focusing my eyes. The clock read four-thirty A.M. "Just a bad dream." I fell back on my pillow. I had to get some rest. The following day was Christmas Eve, and I was scheduled for duty.

I was assigned to a single firehouse that quartered Engine 91, a hose company. In Chicago, firemen work three successive twenty-four-hour shifts, living at the firehouse during that time. I'd have under my command three firefighters and an engineer to monitor the equipment. I was a little nervous. Because of all the holiday leaves, my company had some unseasoned men. I hoped nothing major developed.

By the time I arrived at work the next morning I'd completely forgotten about the dream. In fact, I was happy to find out that my relief engineer had just been promoted, so he must not have been quite as unseasoned as I had feared. Still, I was apprehensive. The holidays are a busy time for firefighters. People get careless during all the excitement. *God*, I prayed, *watch over our city on this wonderful night.*

The shift passed uneventfully. Then, one minute before Christmas, an alarm came in. We manned the engine and roared out of the garage, our siren piercing the night. The blaze was only a half mile from the firehouse, on North Drake Avenue. We were a block away when I spotted smoke. Fire was raging through an old frame house. I called in a second alarm for more equipment and a chief.

We pulled to a stop and I ordered the engineer to hook up both lines and send water through immediately. The first priority was to get the water moving. Then I directed my two other firefighters to grab lines from the hose beds. "Move!" I shouted.

I approached the house. The policeman who had called in the alarm was hammering on the locked front door. "There are people inside," he panted. Through a dingy pane of glass I could dimly see the outline of a body lying in the hallway. "Step back," I told the cop.

I battered my way in. I lifted the body into my arms. It was a woman. She'd probably been overcome by smoke while trying to escape. I wondered if there were kids. Peering through the smoky darkness I could see that the whole downstairs was afire. I was on my way out with the woman when I spotted the second body. It looked like a child's.

Outside, I ordered a firefighter to get the child. I directed another to go in with a line and start fighting the blaze. I put the woman down in a snowbank. Her eyes were fixed and dilated and I could get no carotid pulse. I'd be back to work on her, but first I went to help with the child, a boy of about seven or eight. We put him down next to the woman. He still had a heartbeat.

I started CPR on the woman. It was a cold, icy night, but perspiration streaked from under my helmet. It had taken us only a minute to reach the scene. A person isn't clinically dead until at least six minutes have passed without oxygen, so I figured we had a fair shot at saving this woman.

I tilted her head back, cleared the breathing passage, and gave her five quick breaths followed by fifteen chest compressions. I repeated the steps. No response.

In the background the wail of sirens rose from the night. The firefighter inside called out that the main fire was centered in the front room. I ordered him all the way in to fight it. An instant later I saw one of the hoses a few feet away, bulging from water pressure, snaking rapidly toward the house.

The chief's buggy arrived. The woman still wasn't responding and my efforts were getting frantic. I rubbed snow on her face. "Come on, lady. You can do it."

"What do you have?" the chief snapped as he knelt by my side.

"I've got two people out and one firefighter inside on a line by himself. I need a couple of ambulances."

The chief nodded. Then he peered at the woman. "You'd better give up on her," he said. "She's gone."

"No," I said, pounding her chest. "She still has a chance!" Then, exhausted and frightened, I silently called out: *God, bring her back! I've done all I know how. Only you can help now.* A split second later, I felt her heart pound against my hand. *Thank you, God.*

Sinking back on my heels, I stared up at the blazing structure. *Three people. There were three people in my dream.*

Someone else is in there!

I dashed back into the house. My men would have found any additional victims on the ground floor, so I headed through the smoke toward the stairs. I climbed them slowly, sweeping my flashlight ahead of me. Near the top, I spotted him—a boy lying on his back, unconscious.

He had no carotid pulse. His eyes were dilated. I scooped him up and blew into his mouth, giving him fast cardiac compressions with the fingers of my left hand. I carried him down the steps and outside. As I knelt to lay the boy next to his mother, I felt his heart turn over like a tiny motor. He was alive.

After the fire was out and we were putting away our equipment, the chief returned to the scene from the hospital. He took me aside.

"You did a great job, Captain. But I'm afraid the woman and the little boy aren't going to make it."

"Chief," I said "no one is going to die." I didn't explain about the dream. He wouldn't have believed me.

Christmas morning I called the hospital. All three were stable but suffering from smoke inhalation. I was put through to the woman. I told her I'd been at the scene and asked her what she remembered.

"Well," she said, her voice raspy from the smoke, "I was asleep on the couch when one of the boys started screaming that our Christmas tree was on fire. I tried to get everybody out. The last thing I remember is everything going red. Then it turned to a beautiful white. I heard chanting, like music in church. It was very, very peaceful. Suddenly I saw an older man looking into my face. That's when I woke up outside. They told me one of the older firemen rescued me."

"Ma'am, that was me," I said.

She began thanking me but I cut her short. I told her about the dream. "That dream was a warning, a message not to give up on you and to go back in and find the boy. I didn't save you. God did."

That's all I wanted to say. I wasn't the hero. I'd been told what to do on Christmas Eve when I was awakened by the most vivid dream of my life. In a sense, like all good firefighters, I was just following orders.

His Mysterious Ways

MY FAMILY AND I lived on a farm in the mountains of Virginia, and for many years my mother made her home with us. But one morning Mother woke up completely disoriented, and during the years that followed, she grew progressively worse. Her ability to communicate with anyone was gone. I felt numb about her silent condition. It was as though she were lost to us and, it seemed to me, lost to God as well.

On the day before Christmas Eve, some carolers came over the hills. The group of young people—led by Miss Winnie and Miss Naomi, two missionaries from our church, and our pastor's wife Phyllis—sang in the snow outside our door. Then I hustled everyone into our big, warm kitchen for hot chocolate and cookies. I took the three ladies into Mother's room, and Phyllis leaned over the bed and said, "Grandmother, it's Christmas."

No response.

Phyllis took her hand and said again, "Grandmother, do you know what Christmas is?"

Then it happened. Mother's eyes flew open, and it was as if a light had been turned on behind them. An angelic smile spread over her worn features; and in a strong, normal voice she replied, "Oh, yes! It is the birthday of my precious Savior."

Now we eagerly plied Mother with questions, but it was over. Those were the last words that Mother ever spoke, but they were enough. I knew beyond a shadow of a doubt that the birth of Jesus Christ has a power beyond anything we can consciously comprehend, and that Mother was in his hands forever.

—BETTY BANNER, *December 1983*

Mystery of the Hatbox Baby

SHARON ELLIOTT

December 1993

M om's voice on the phone was urgent. "Can you take a few days off to come see me? We have to talk."

"Sure, Mom. But why wait? Let's talk now."

"Not over the phone, Sharon. Come see me soon. Please."

I was fifty-five and living in California at the time, and my mother and I had always been close. I dropped everything and flew to Arizona.

As soon as I saw Mom, I could tell that her health was getting worse. She and I sat on the couch. "There is something I've never told you," she said, her frail hands shaking as she put a packet in my lap. Puzzled, I opened the large brown envelope and pulled out a stack of yellowed newspaper clippings.

> Mystery still surrounds the "Hatbox Baby," found abandoned in the desert on Christmas Eve, 1931.

What was this all about? I kept reading.

> The finding of the six-day-old infant not only touched
> off a mystery; it was considered almost miraculous.
>
> She was swaddled in old cotton wrappings. A hat-
> box was her crib. Investigators said it was surely a
> miracle that she had not died in the cold or been
> devoured by prowling coyotes.
>
> But strange things happen at Christmas.

I was starting to feel very strange myself. I read on, scanning
headline after headline. In 1931: "Foundling to Get New Home."
Then from a column years later: "State's Christmas Baby Miracle
of the Desert." And from a major feature article in Parade magazine in 1961: "Where is the Hatbox Baby Today?"

"Mom?"

My mother took both my hands in hers, her eyes full of tears.
"It's you, Sharon. You were that baby."

I stared at her in disbelief. Until this moment I had had no
idea that I was adopted. Over the next hours, Mom told me the
incredible story.

At sundown on Christmas Eve, 1931, an Arizona couple was
driving home across a barren stretch of desert some forty miles
out of Mesa when they developed car trouble. While the husband
worked to repair a broken fuel line, the wife walked away from
the road, wandering under the glittering stars among the cacti,
rocks, and sagebrush. And then she caught sight of something in
a clump of bushes.

It was a round, black hatbox, its top not tightly closed. The
woman called her husband, who prodded the box gently with his

foot. They heard a cry and opened the lid. Inside was a baby—a baby with red hair and blue eyes.

The astonished couple took the baby into town to the Mesa police station and gave her to the deputy sheriff on duty; he took the baby to a maternity home run by a midwife named "Ma" Dana. The next morning, investigators returned to the desert to search for anything that might identify the infant. There was nothing.

Word of the "hatbox baby" spread rapidly. "I heard the news on the radio that Christmas morning," Mom said. "I'd always longed for a baby, but I had never been able to carry one to term. So I shut off the oven without a thought of the turkey cooking inside, and we rushed out to get our names on the list to adopt you."

> Found in the desert a week ago, the baby must depend
> on the law to give her a mother and father to succeed
> those who deserted her to die in a cheap hatbox.

Mom stroked my red hair. "By the time the court date came two months later," she said, "more than two hundred couples had signed up to adopt you. I figured we didn't stand much chance, but I prayed and prayed. The night before the hearing, it rained so hard that the bridge into town washed out, and most of the streets were flooded. Only one other couple was able to get to the courthouse—and since they already had an adopted child, the judge awarded you to us."

"I'm so glad you were the ones who got me," I whispered, clinging to my mother the way I had as a child when something was wrong. I loved her dearly—I always would. But now I was an adult, and once again something was wrong, involving deep emotions I wasn't yet ready to examine.

I took the packet of clippings with me when I left that night. I tried not to think about them. But Mom's failing health concerned me. She was alone; my stepfather had died several years ago. I was divorced, so I decided to retire from my job as an aerospace worker and move back to Mesa to be with Mom. Eight months later she died.

Her death filled me with grief. But one night as I stared out at the desert hills, I began to be haunted by other thoughts. I opened that packet again and read the newspaper clippings.

> It is surely a miracle that the baby had not been devoured by prowling coyotes or wolves, and that she didn't die of cold.

Had my birth mother really left me to die? Was I so unacceptable that she'd rejected me completely, discarding me without a thought in such a barren, lonely place?

I'd heard that many adopted children, no matter how adored, still longed for assurance that they'd been worthy and wanted as newborns. My rational mind said, "You're an adult now; it doesn't matter." But on some deeper level it mattered terribly. Had my real mother not cared whether I lived or died? *Please, God*, I prayed, *send some word to comfort me.*

Then, with the help of Orphan Voyage, an organization that tries to reunite adopted children with their birth parents, I searched for more information. I learned that "Ma" Dana was now dead, and the couple that had found me had long ago left the area.

But what about the deputy sheriff on duty the night I was found? His name was in the old articles—Joe Maier.

Was he alive? And still somewhere in the area? I could hardly believe it when I found a listing for Joe B. Maier in the phone book.

I was shaking as I walked up to a frame house and rang the bell. Joe Maier was a friendly, big man with white hair and a keen gaze, and he took my hand in a warm grasp. It turned out he'd stayed on the force and become police chief in Mesa for a number of years. Now in his nineties, he lived with his daughter. And he remembered the night in 1931 very well.

"Not a Christmas Eve goes by that I don't think of it," he said. "For years folks wondered what happened to the hatbox baby, and now here you are."

His daughter brought us tea as we sat in their cozy living room. "Mesa was a small town then, and the people here all fell in love with you," Joe said. "They showered you with gifts." On Christmas day at "Ma" Dana's, he told me, folks from miles around brought shawls and dresses and booties, and a jeweler sent a ring and a locket. Joe's kind eyes twinkled as he talked. "In a way, it reminded us of that very first Christmas. You were a gift to all of us."

I struggled to tell him how I felt. "It's been really hard for me," I said, "to think I was just . . . dumped in the desert to die."

Joe Maier shook his head. "No way," he said firmly. "You were clean, in a tidy flowered sleeper, with a blanket around you. You were in good shape, you'd been well cared for, and it's clear you couldn't have been out in the desert for long."

He leaned forward. "There are a lot of questions about

where you came from that night, questions that may never be answered. God knows, a lot of folks had theories about what did and didn't happen."

His steady gaze never wavered. "Was somebody hiding in the sagebrush watching to make sure you'd be found? Was that good-hearted couple who brought you in telling us the whole story? Nobody knows for sure. But this much I am certain of: the baby put into my hands was clean and well cared for—and was meant to be found and given a good home."

I said goodbye to Joe with a sense of peace I hadn't had for months. That night I reread a letter my mom had written me before she died, describing the first time she saw me—"a little redheaded mite, so perfect and so perfectly adorable." Mom said she felt that maybe women like her, who loved children so much but couldn't give birth, were created to care for those babies who didn't have mothers.

Left in the middle of nowhere? No, none of us are. And maybe that baby in Bethlehem was born to let us know.

Strange things can happen at Christmas, in a desert under the stars.

"I Knew You Would Come"

ELIZABETH KING ENGLISH

December 1995

Herman and I locked our store and dragged ourselves home to South Caldwell Street. It was eleven P.M., Christmas Eve of 1949. We were dog-tired.

Ours was one of those big, old general appliance stores that sold everything from refrigerators, toasters, and record players to bicycles, dollhouses, and games. We had sold almost all of our toys; and all of the layaways, except one package, had been picked up.

Usually Herman and I kept the store open until everything had been claimed. We wouldn't have woken up happy on Christmas morning knowing that some child's gift was still on the layaway shelf. But the person who had put a dollar down on that package never returned.

Early Christmas morning our twelve-year-old son, Tom, and Herman and I were around the tree opening gifts. But there was something humdrum about this Christmas. Tom was growing up; he had wanted just clothes and games. I missed his childish exuberance of past years.

As soon as breakfast was over, Tom left to visit his friend next door. Herman mumbled, "I'm going back to sleep. There's nothing left to stay up for."

So there I was alone, doing the dishes and feeling let down. It was nearly nine A.M., and sleet mixed with snow cut the air outside. The wind rattled our windows, and I felt grateful for the warmth of the apartment. *Sure glad I don't have to go out on a day like today*, I thought, picking up the wrapping paper and ribbons strewn around the living room.

And then it began—something I had never experienced before, a strange, persistent urge. It seemed to be telling me to go to the store.

I looked at the icy sidewalk outside. *That's crazy*, I said to myself. I tried dismissing the urge, but it wouldn't leave me alone. In fact, it was getting stronger.

Well, I wasn't going to go. I had never gone to the store on Christmas Day in all the ten years we had owned it. No one opened shop on that day. There wasn't any reason to go, I didn't want to, and I wasn't going to.

For an hour I fought that strange feeling. Finally, I couldn't stand it any longer, and I got dressed.

"Herman," I said, feeling silly, "I think I'll walk down to the store."

Herman woke with a start. "Whatever for? What are you going to do there?"

"Oh, I don't know," I replied lamely. "There's not much to do here. I just think I'll wander down."

He argued against it a little, but I told him that I would be back soon. "Well, go on," he grumped, "but I don't see any reason for it."

I put on my gray wool coat and tam, then my galoshes, red scarf, and gloves. Once outside, none of those garments seemed to help. The wind cut right through me and the sleet stung my cheeks. I groped my way the mile down to 117 East Park Avenue, slipping and sliding.

I shivered and tucked my hands inside my pockets to keep them from freezing. I felt ridiculous. I had no business being out in that bitter chill.

There was the store just ahead. In front of it stood two boys, one about nine and the other six. *What in the world?* I wondered.

"Here she comes!" yelled the older one. He had his arm around the younger. "See, I told you she would come," he said jubilantly.

They were half frozen. The younger one's face was wet with tears, but when he saw me, his eyes opened wide and his sobbing stopped.

"What are you two children doing out here in this freezing rain?" I scolded, hurrying them into the store and turning up the heat. "You should be at home on a day like this!" They were poorly dressed. They had no hats or gloves, and their shoes barely held together. I rubbed their small, icy hands, and got them up close to the heater.

"We've been waiting for you," replied the older boy. He told me that they had been standing outside since nine A.M., the time I normally opened the store.

"Why were you waiting for me?" I asked, astonished.

"My little brother Jimmy didn't get any Christmas." He touched Jimmy's shoulder. "We want to buy some skates. That's what he wants. We have these three dollars. See, Miss Lady," he said, pulling the bills from his pocket.

I looked at the money in his hand. I looked at their expectant faces. And then I looked around the store. "I'm sorry," I said, "but we've sold almost everything. We have no—" Then my eye caught sight of the layaway shelf with its lone package.

"Wait a minute," I told the boys. I walked over, picked up the package, and unwrapped it. Miraculously, there was a pair of skates!

Jimmy reached for them. *Lord*, I prayed silently, *let them be his size.*

And, miracle added upon miracle, they were his size.

When the older boy finished tying the laces on Jimmy's right skate and saw that it fit—perfectly—he stood up and presented the three dollars to me.

"No, I'm not going to take your money," I told him. I couldn't take his money. "I want you to have these skates, and I want you to use your money to get some gloves."

The boys just blinked at first. Then their eyes became like saucers, and their grins stretched wide when they understood I was giving them the skates.

What I saw in Jimmy's eyes was like a blessing. It was pure joy, and it was beautiful. My spirits rose.

After the children had warmed up, I turned down the heater, and we walked out together. As I locked the door, I turned to the older brother and said, "How lucky that I happened to come along when I did. If you had stood there much longer, you would have frozen. But how did you boys know I would come?"

I wasn't prepared for his reply. His gaze was steady, and he answered me softly. "I knew you would come," he said. "I asked Jesus to send you."

The tingles in my spine weren't from the cold, I knew. God had planned this.

As we waved goodbye, I turned home to a brighter Christmas than I had left. Tom brought his friend over to our house. Herman got out of bed; his father, "Papa" English, and sister Ella came by. We had a delicious dinner and a wonderful time.

But the one thing that made that Christmas really joyous was the one thing that makes every Christmas wonderful—Jesus was there.

The Spark of Life

SHARON ATWELL

December 2002

elcome home, baby girl," I said to our youngest, thirteen-year-old Katelyn, trying to keep my voice from wavering despite what the doctors at St. Jude had told me before we left the hospital. Their words replayed in my mind, a terrible echo that refused to fade away: "It's not a matter of if she dies, but when."

It was late, two A.M., on Christmas; and the house was quiet except for the faint mechanical sigh of Kate's oxygen pump and the beeps of the machines that tracked her heart rate and breathing. My husband, Ray, and our older daughter, Crystal, had finally gone to bed, but I couldn't bring myself to leave Kate. Not just yet. Not with the knowledge that when morning came she might no longer be with us.

Kate had been at St. Jude, the renowned children's research hospital, getting treatment for leukemia, when the *Bacillus cereus* infection attacked her brain. Only six cases of this deadly meningitis had ever been documented. Kate had slipped into a coma, but she'd hung on for five months. I'd taken her survival as a sign: The same never-give-up spirit that had driven her as a competitive swimmer and won her a place as the only sixth-grader on her middle school flag team still burned. "Our Kate is still here," I insisted. "She's trying to break through. She needs us."

We would hug her as if she could hug us back, talk to her as if she could hear us, play her favorite music. I made sure to paint her nails the way she liked, with a polish that said "Hello, world!" even if she couldn't. Blue glitter, maybe, or candy-apple red. I told everyone, "One of these days something we're doing will get through to her." I believed that with all my heart. Even if her muscles had wasted away, even if she looked nothing like the girl who used to power through swim practice and put away half a pizza afterward, I wasn't ready for Kate to die. If that was what the Lord wanted, he would have made me ready.

Then they hit—what the specialists called autonomic storms. Kate's autonomic nervous system, which regulates heartbeat, respiration, and other basic functions necessary for life, went haywire, skyrocketing her temperature to 109 degrees, her pulse to 240, her blood pressure to 185/135. The storms would subside occasionally, but that was even scarier. Kate's pulse would slow until there was such a long lull between heartbeats that I'd find myself pleading, "Come on, baby girl, come on, Lord, one more time!" Finally, after a week and a half, her medical team told me, "There's not much more her body can take. You need to decide whether you want Kate to spend her last days at home."

It was the hardest talk our family had ever had. We all wanted to be together in one place, instead of how we'd been living—me keeping a vigil at Kate's side in the ICU, Ray shuttling between the hospital and the Mazda plant where he's a supervisor, Crystal holding down the home front when she should have been enjoying her junior year in high school. But I'd forced myself to ask, "Can we handle bringing Kate home only to have her die?"

Crystal hadn't hesitated for a second. "Things aren't going to go that way," she'd declared. "Bring Kate home. Let God show everyone what he can do."

I tugged the blanket over Kate's arms, my heart aching at how they were drawn up like withered branches. Were we doing the right thing? What if her windpipe got clogged and I couldn't clear her trach tube? What if her heart stopped beating after the next storm? My head was still reeling from the crash course the ICU staff had given me on her day-to-day care—including twenty-seven medications that had to be administered at specific times—never mind emergencies. I tucked the blanket around her shoulders. "I love you, Kate," I said—our nightly ritual since she was little. I had to leave before I blurted out, *Please, God, don't let this be the last time.*

I crawled into bed beside Ray, but I could only doze, keeping one ear tuned to the baby monitor we'd hooked up to Kate's room, the other to the clock that would buzz when it was time for the next medication. I was up before the alarm sounded at six o'clock Christmas morning.

Crystal put up the tree and played CDs of the carols we would have sung at church, but it was a subdued Christmas. I wasn't up to doing much of anything except checking on Kate, morning, noon, and night. Ray tried to coax me into letting myself rest; but how could I, when each hour might be my daughter's last?

Two days passed. Three. Four. Every time I stepped out of Kate's room I was terrified that she would slip away before I got back. I felt trapped between desperation and desolation. *Not if, but when she dies*, the hopeless prognosis resounded in my thoughts. *When she dies*. Was God using this time to prepare me to let my baby girl go? One night I fell into Ray's arms and broke down. "I can't go on like this, waiting for Kate to die."

"Maybe we don't have to," he said quietly. "I keep thinking about those folks from Holly Springs. Nurse Marilyn . . ."

Had it been only this summer that the men from Holly Springs walked into our lives? We'd been through so much that it seemed like ages ago. In late June Kate had developed a backache that wouldn't go away. Diagnosed with leukemia, she'd begun treatment at St. Jude. "I'll look like Tweety Bird after chemo: big eyes and no hair," she told her friends, with her trademark pluck and humor. "But that's okay. It's going to help me get better." High-dose chemo can wipe out the immune system, so when she complained of a bad headache, her doctor put her on antibiotics and admitted her to the hospital. On July 14 Kate suffered a massive seizure. She didn't regain consciousness. Deadly *Bacillus cereus* meningitis had laid siege to her weakened system.

The next morning a top neurosurgeon studied Kate's charts and CAT scan. "There is no hope for her," he informed us.

Ray, Crystal, and I weren't ready to believe that. Neither was the ICU doctor. He called in another specialist, neurosurgeon Stephanie Einhaus from the Semmes-Murphey Clinic. "No one

knows much about this type of meningitis, so I may have to figure things out as I go along," she said. "I promise I'll do everything I can."

Yes, this is what we need for Kate, I'd wanted to shout. *People
who see the possible. Lord, keep them coming!*

He sure had—our family and friends; the staff at St. Jude and
Dr. Einhaus; Pastor Sam and everyone else at Germantown
Baptist; and most awe-inspiring of all, total strangers. One
Wednesday night two men showed up at St. Jude, a pastor and a
deacon from a little church in Holly Springs, Mississippi. At their
evening worship, one of Ray's workers at Mazda had requested
prayers for Kate, and right afterward these gentlemen drove an
hour and a half to see us. "God has his hand on your little girl,"
they said. "He's going to pull her through this. Just stand strong
in your faith."

Then there was the nurse named Marilyn who'd sought us
out in the ICU on December 14. She didn't work at St. Jude, but
at Le Bonheur, the hospital where Dr. Einhaus did Kate's brain
surgeries. She presented us with a blanket she'd had one hundred
nurses lay hands on and pray over. "To help cover Katelyn with
prayer," she said. Then she added, "I feel like I'm supposed to tell
you: Things are going to get really bad. But they will get better,
and so will she." That very same day, the autonomic storms
struck Kate.

I held Ray close, letting those memories he'd called to mind
warm me as surely as his embrace. How could I have let my fears
make me lose sight of the messages we'd gotten from strangers
and loved ones alike? Together they added up to one mighty

promise from God. Forget waiting for my daughter to die. Trusting the Lord's promise, trusting that Katelyn would live—that was how I'd gotten through those long, uncertain months in the hospital, and that's how I would go on now.

New Year's Eve we all dressed up—I chose a festive outfit for Kate—and went to church with IV, pumps, and all. It felt so good to be in God's house again. In our own house, in Kate's room, her favorite CDs went back on heavy rotation. I put up a map and marked every city where we knew someone was praying for her. "When you wake up, baby girl, you're going to be amazed to see how many people prayed you well."

I started sending "Kate Update" e-mails to everyone on that map, as much to remind me as to keep them posted of all our prayers that were being answered: like the used van we got that had a lift for Kate's wheelchair, so we could take her everywhere, even prom-dress shopping with Crystal; like the day her doctor at St. Jude called to set up appointments for checkups and physical therapy—he hadn't scheduled any when we left because he didn't think Kate would still be around; like the times she would turn her head toward our voices.

In March, Kate had another brain surgery. "Don't worry," Dr. Einhaus said. "I see miracles all the time." Sure enough, after Kate got home from the hospital, she began to make facial expressions—an "icky" face when I swabbed a bad-tasting medication in her mouth. We found a wonderful night nurse who lived just two blocks away. Boy, once I got a full night's sleep, it was a lot easier to stay positive.

Not that Kate didn't give me good reason. She made one step

forward after another, nodding yes or no, following simple commands, sleeping without her oxygen pump, telling me what she wanted (one finger for food, two fingers for drink). Our friends had us over to their pool every day that summer, and Crystal did a great job exercising Kate's arms and legs in the water. Kate still couldn't talk or see, but she got strong enough to blow kisses to her daddy and hug her big sister.

Sometimes she'd get frustrated at her slow progress in physical therapy. But I had only to say, "Remember how many laps you used to swim in practice just to knock two-tenths of a second off your race time?" Kate would nod and get right back to her exercises. At Christmas she had come home to die. Now she was fighting to live again.

One night in late September, I leaned over to tuck her in like always. "I love you, Kate," I said. When I straightened up, what did I see but Kate saying to me, mouthing the words perfectly, "I love you too." The big goofy grin didn't leave my face for days. Pretty soon Kate was lip-synching to her CDs and telling everyone, "My God is awesome!"

Kate's mental and physical progress astounded doctors. Her sight came back just in time for her fourteenth birthday, November 20. "One day Kate will be typing the update herself," I e-mailed everyone after the party. "That's a God thing." In December, Kate was eating real food, including her favorite meal, pizza, and celebrating Christmas with all our family in Florida— the same girl that doctors had sent home just a year before, never expecting to see her alive again. Like she says, God is awesome!

He keeps giving us moments to remember. On May 18, 2001,

at Crystal's high-school graduation, Kate crossed the stage with her. On September 18, Kate had her last chemo treatment. December 14, Kate wheeled through downtown Memphis, carrying the Olympic torch. On February 5, 2002, Kate graduated—to a walker. July 16, Kate swam with dolphins, thanks to the Make-a-Wish Foundation.

And one of my favorites is August 12, Kate's first day of school in three years. I watched, awestruck, as she walked into her new high school. My baby girl is growing up and growing stronger, moving boldly into her future. And I can only marvel at how, when you live not in fear but in hope, trusting God completely, taking step after step with your hand in his, every day is a miracle.

A Puppy Named Maxx

Suzan Davis

December 2004

As soon as my daughters and I walked into the house, they started in on me again. "So, Mom, can we get a dog?" Katelyn, thirteen, said.

"Yeah, Mom," Savannah, eleven, echoed. "Pleeease?"

They'd been after me for weeks. I'd even overheard them asking for a puppy in their bedtime prayers. The last thing in the world I wanted to do was disappoint my daughters, but I was a busy single mom. I had enough on my plate. "C'mon, you guys," I said, glancing at the answering machine. The message light was blinking. "We already have a dog."

Duke, our beagle-corgi mix, lifted his head from his bed, as if he knew we were talking about him. Good old Duke. At six, he was as sweet as could be, but not exactly a bundle of energy. He hardly ever got up to greet us anymore.

"We need a dog we can play with, Mom," Katelyn said. "A puppy. This family isn't big enough."

I felt a pang of guilt. I'd promised myself that the girls wouldn't miss out on anything after their dad and I were separated. My teaching schedule at a local college gave me plenty of time to be with my daughters, and I thought I'd done a pretty good job raising them. Still, doubts had a way of creeping in. Especially now, with the holidays around the corner. Everyone else was planning big family get-togethers. It was just me and my girls. Could I really give them everything they needed?

"Maybe Santa will bring us a puppy next month," said Savannah hopefully.

"A Chihuahua," Katelyn added. "Like in *Legally Blonde*."

"Now *that* I draw the line at," I said. "There are too many coyotes around here. If we do get a dog, it's got to be bigger than a dinner entree." I hit the play button on the answering machine.

The message was from our neighbor. "Hi, Suzan. Want a dog?"

The girls whooped and hollered. I was trapped. How could I say no? Our neighbor was always rescuing animals. This time, it turned out to be a German shepherd. The girls forgot all about Chihuahuas and immediately dubbed him Wolfgang Gunter Klaus von Schneiderheim—Wolfie for short.

Wolfie wasn't with us a week before I was every bit as in love with him as the girls were. Who knew I'd take such pleasure in being followed around by this floppy-eared goofball with his funny, lopsided gait? He'd trail me from room to room, out to the front gate to get the mail, everywhere. Even Duke seemed to approve of the new arrival, thumping his tail whenever Wolfie came over to give him a sniff. Wolfie didn't like being separated from us for a second, so I took him with me to work at the college.

Like some of my students, he didn't take notes and had a tendency to fall asleep during my lectures. Yes, it was my daughters who had prayed for a puppy, but Wolfie ended up filling a space in my life too. *Lord, thank you for sending Wolfie to complete our family.*

A few weeks before Christmas, Wolfie's odd gait turned into a pronounced limp. And he was only picking at his food. I took him to the veterinarian.

He gave Wolfie a full exam and took x-rays. "This is bad, Suzan," he said. "I noticed Wolfie's hips were narrow. This x-ray shows why. Wolfie was born without any hip sockets. His back legs are poking into him whenever he walks. He's in constant pain. That's why he's not eating. We'll get a second opinion, but don't expect it to be good news."

It wasn't. The only humane thing to do, the other vets I consulted informed me, was to put Wolfie down. As unexpectedly as he had come into our lives, Wolfie would be leaving us.

On December 15, Wolfie passed away peacefully, snuggled in Savannah's and my arms. The girls and I cried a bucket of tears. I did my best to make Christmas a happy one for my daughters, but it was no use. Wolfie's absence cast a pall over everything.

I thought that a day out at a shopping center—we'd have a nice lunch then hit the after-Christmas sales—might cheer them up. But outside one store there was a line of SPCA cages full of dogs that needed homes. Savannah picked up a puppy and held it close, as if trying to fill the hole left by Wolfie's loss.

Katelyn couldn't even look at the dogs. "Mom, can we get out of here?" she pleaded. "They all just remind me of Wolfie."

Lord, I prayed, *I thought Wolfie was supposed to complete our family. Now what am I going to do?*

Halfway home, my cell phone rang. It was a young woman named Dana Swain, the leader of a Girl Scout troop in town.

"Suzan, I found your dog."

Our dog?

"I'm sorry, Dana, what did you say?"

"He was standing in the middle of Auburn-Folsom Road with cars whizzing by on both sides. But don't worry, I got him. I'll drop him off. Inside your fence, so he can't get out again."

Auburn-Folsom Road was a full mile from our house. How had sleepy old Duke mustered the energy to get that far? We pulled up to our house. Sure enough, there was a dog standing behind the fence.

Not Duke. A wet, muddy German shepherd puppy.

"He looks just like Wolfie!" Savannah cried. "Are we in the twilight zone?"

We walked through the gate and the puppy jumped on the girls, covering them with licks. I opened our front door. The puppy charged into the house without a moment's pause. He sniffed Duke (who didn't seem to mind), then sat and looked up at me expectantly. I set out some water and food. He inhaled the kibble so quickly the girls burst into peals of laughter.

I called Dana and told her this couldn't be our dog because we'd had to put Wolfie down. "I'm sorry, I had no idea," she said. "When I saw that shepherd puppy in the middle of the road, I figured it had to be yours."

It was easy to see why. He could have been Wolfie's twin. If we were in the twilight zone, like Savannah said, for the moment I didn't care. After weeks of sadness, our house was full of joy again.

Not for long. Early the next morning, Dana called again. "I hate to tell you, but I saw a sign at the market just now, about a lost four-month-old shepherd." She gave me the owner's number.

I forced myself to dial it. This call was going to break my daughter's hearts.

"Oh, I'm so glad you have my dog," the woman said. "I'll be right over."

I went into the girls' room. They were asleep, with the already christened Noah Maximillion von Swain, or Maxx, curled up at the foot of Katelyn's bed.

I woke the girls and broke the news. "The owner will be here soon," I said.

"Mom," Savannah said, "I've got almost nine hundred dollars saved up in my bank account. Do you think if I give it to the lady she'll let us keep Maxx?"

"Honey, it's not about the money. It's about where the dog belongs."

Savannah turned and buried her face in Maxx's neck.

The owner arrived. Katelyn and Savannah watched, not saying a word, as she threw her arms around Maxx.

"Thank you so much," she said. "This dog wasn't at my house an hour before he ran away."

Maxx padded over to my daughters and plopped down between them.

"We had a German shepherd," said Katelyn. "Just like this one. He died right before Christmas."

The woman looked at the dog and my two girls for a long moment.

"I wanted an eight-week-old female," she said. "But somehow yesterday I found myself buying this four-month-old male. I put him in the backyard, and an hour later he'd vanished. My fence has held plenty of dogs over the years. Not one of them ever got out. I couldn't understand it. Well, now I do. This puppy was looking for the right family. And he's found it. You know, I think God chose him for you."

I think so too. We single mothers take all the help we can get. Did I say I was raising my daughters all on my own? Not by a long shot.

Christmas Angels

The Host of Heaven

DR. S. RALPH HARLOW

December 1963

*I*t was not Christmas, it was not even wintertime, when
the event occurred that for me threw sudden, new light on
the ancient angel tale. It was a glorious spring morning, and we
were walking, my wife and I, through the newly budded birches
and maples near Ballardvale, Massachusetts.

Now I realize that this, like any account of personal experience, is only as valid as the good sense and honesty of the person
relating it. What can I say about myself? That I am a scholar who
shuns guesswork and admires scientific investigation? That I have
an AB from Harvard, an MA from Columbia, a PhD from Hartford
Theological Seminary? That I have never been subject to halluci-
nations? That attorneys have solicited my testimony, and I have
testified in the courts, regarded by judge and jury as a faithful,
reliable witness? All this is true, and yet I doubt that any amount
of such credentials can influence the belief or disbelief of another.

In the long run, each of us must sift what comes to us from

others through his or her own life experience, view of the universe, and understanding. And so I will simply tell my story.

The little path on which Marion and I walked that morning was spongy to our steps. We held hands, with sheer delight in life, as we strolled near a lovely brook. It was May; and because it was the examination reading period for students at Smith College where I was a professor, we were able to get away for a few days to visit Marion's parents.

We frequently took walks in the country; we especially loved the spring after a hard New England winter, for it is then that the fields and the woods are radiant and calm yet show new life bursting from the earth. This day we were especially happy and peaceful; we chatted sporadically, with great gaps of satisfying silence between our sentences.

Then from behind us we heard the murmur of muted voices in the distance, and I said to Marion, "We have company in the woods this morning."

Marion nodded and turned to look. We saw nothing, but the voices were coming nearer—at a faster pace than we were walking, and we knew that the strangers would soon overtake us. Then we perceived that the sounds were not only behind us but above us, and we looked up.

How can I describe what we felt? Is it possible to tell of the surge of exaltation that ran through us? Is it possible to record this phenomenon with objective accuracy and yet be credible?

For about ten feet above us, and slightly to our left, was a floating group of glorious, beautiful creatures that glowed with spiritual beauty. We stopped and stared as they passed above us.

There were six of them—young, beautiful women dressed in flowing white garments and engaged in earnest conversation. If they were aware of our existence, they gave no indication of it. Their faces were perfectly clear to us; and one woman, slightly older than the rest, was especially beautiful. Her dark hair was pulled back in what today we would call a ponytail; and although I cannot say it was bound at the back of her head, it appeared to be. She was talking intently to a younger spirit whose back was toward us and who looked up into the face of the woman who was talking.

Neither Marion nor I could understand their words, although their voices were clearly heard. The sound was somewhat like hearing but being unable to understand a group of people talking outside a house with all the windows and doors shut.

They seemed to float past us, and their graceful motion seemed natural—as gentle and peaceful as the morning itself. As they passed, their conversation grew fainter and fainter until it faded out entirely. We stood transfixed on the spot, still holding hands and still with the vision before our eyes.

It would be an understatement to say that we were astounded. Then we looked at each other, each wondering if the other also had seen.

There was a fallen birch tree just there beside the path. We sat down on it and I said, "Marion, what did you see? Tell me exactly, in precise detail. And tell me what you heard."

She knew my intent—to test my own eyes and ears, to see if I had been the victim of hallucination or imagination. And her reply was identical in every respect to what my own senses had reported to me.

I have related this story with the same faithfulness and respect for truth and accuracy as I would employ on the witness stand. But even as I record it, I know how incredible it sounds.

Perhaps I can claim no more for it than that it has had a deep effect on our own lives. For this experience of almost thirty years ago greatly altered our thinking. Once, both Marion and I had been somewhat skeptical about the absolute accuracy of the details of the birth of Christ. The story, as recorded by Luke, tells of an angel appearing to shepherds abiding in the field; and after the shepherds had been told of the birth, "suddenly there was with the angel a multitude of the heavenly host praising God, and saying, Glory to God in the highest. . . ."

As a child I accepted the multitude seen by the shepherds as literal heavenly personages. Then I went through a period when I felt that they were merely symbols injected into a fantasy or legend. Today, after the experience at Ballardvale, Marion and I are no longer skeptical. We believe that in back of that story recorded by Luke lies a genuine, objective experience told in wonder by those who had the experience.

Once, too, we puzzled greatly over the Christian insistence that we have "bodies" other than our normal flesh and blood ones. We were like the doubter of whom Paul wrote in 1 Corinthians 15: "But some man will say, How are the dead raised up? and with what body do they come?"

In the thirty years since that bright May morning, his answer has rung for us with joyous conviction.

There are also celestial bodies, and bodies terrestrial: but the glory of the celestial is one, and the glory of the terrestrial is another. . . . So also is the resurrection of the dead. . . . It is sown a natural body; it is raised a spiritual body. . . . And as we have borne the image of the earthy, we shall also bear the image of the heavenly. . . . For this corruptible must put on incorruption, and this mortal must put on immortality (1 Corinthians 15:40–53).

All of us, I think, hear the angels for a little while at Christmastime. We let the heavenly host come close once a year. But we reject the very possibility that what the shepherds saw two thousand years ago was part of the reality that presses close every day of our lives.

And yet there is no reason for us to shrink from this knowledge. Since Marion and I began to be aware of the host of heaven all about us, our lives have been filled with a wonderful hope. Phillips Brooks, the great Episcopal bishop, expressed the cause of this hope more beautifully than I can do:

This is what you are to hold fast to yourself—the sympathy and companionship of the unseen worlds. No doubt it is best for us now that they should be unseen. It cultivates in us that higher perception that we call 'faith.' But who can say that the time will not come when, even to those who live here upon earth, the unseen worlds shall no longer be unseen?

The experience at Ballardvale, added to the convictions of my Christian faith, gives me not only a feeling of assurance about the future, but a sense of adventure toward it too.

Angel Cups

LUCY MEYER

December 1972

Ten years ago I worked in a small television station which was owned and operated by a large parent station two hundred miles away. My job was to write copy for local commercials. That year, as the Christmas season advanced, the repetition of writing "buy this" and "buy that" got me down. It was the strongest dose of the wrong side of Christmas I had ever experienced.

One night at home I mulled over the copy I had written that day; and there, all alone, I began to talk to God. "Oh, Lord," I said, "if only there was something in my job about a Christmas gift you didn't have to buy, something with no strings, no profits, no angles, no ten percent down. Just for love." For several days this yearning deepened within me.

Christmas Eve afternoon we had a quiet employees' party in the office kitchen. We were all standing together in a little knot of self-conscious festivity when Mr. Barstow, from our parent station, passed a brightly wrapped present to each of us. Everyone received the same gift, a cheery coffee mug with an amusing little angel face on it and the employee's name labeled in gold beneath. When I opened mine, I noticed the mistake immediately. The name "Anna" was on my cup.

"They've given you the wrong one," Mr. Barstow said apologetically. "That's for one of the girls in bookkeeping back in the home office. And she probably has yours. Listen, I'll take it back with me now and I'll have yours shipped to you right away."

It seemed to me that Mr. Barstow was overly concerned about the matter. "That's too much trouble," I protested. "I don't mind having Anna's if she doesn't mind having mine."

"No, I want to straighten it out. It's important. Anna's in the hospital."

"What's the matter?" Janet, our traffic-log girl, asked.

"She's paralyzed," Mr. Barstow told us. He didn't know the medical details, but Anna was in serious condition.

The party picked up again, and we all had coffee in the new cups. Yet I hesitated. I felt superstitious about drinking from Anna's cup. After a few sips, I put it down.

When I went to bed that Christmas Eve, I easily fell asleep. It had been a hectic day. But in the middle of the night, I awakened suddenly, sharply, to one of the strangest experiences of my life. As I lay there fully awake, an inexplicable feeling of grief washed over me. I did not know why, but tears started rolling down my cheeks and as I tried to take my hands to wipe them away, I found to my shock that my arms would not move. I could not lift them.

In a single wave of remembrance, I recalled the angel cup. Anna's cup. Now I wept uncontrollably. "God," I prayed out loud, and the words seemed to come not so much from me as from an outside force, "help her!" Again I tried to raise my arms. They were glued to my sides. "Look, look, God, that's the way it is with Anna. She can't even raise her arms to pray. Help her."

More and more I went on. I was praying in a fashion unlike myself, praying outside my own efforts, like a fountain pouring from an unknown source. Part of me seemed to stand aside, watching and listening in amazement. Gradually my arms lost their heaviness, and slowly I found I could raise them—up, up, up. How good it felt! Now my prayer became one of thanksgiving, and as suddenly as it had come, the grief left me. The tears stopped. I fell asleep.

I was off Christmas Day, but when I returned to the office it fell to my lot to take the regular afternoon hot-line phone call from the parent studio. My little office was filled with people. The six o'clock news announcer was checking his copy. The manager was shouting at the cameraman to use the number two camera for the jewelry commercial due on the screen in ten minutes. One of the engineers stood by my desk ready to talk as soon as I finished. But just before I relinquished the phone, I asked, "How is Anna?"

"She's better. Just all of a sudden, in the early hours of Christmas, she could move her arms and legs again. It . . . well . . . it was really strange."

"How wonderful," I said quietly, wildly excited inside.

"Wasn't it a marvelous Christmas gift for her!"

"Yes. What a marvelous Christmas gift," I said, and I gave the phone over to the impatient engineer. Surrounded by the noise and pressure of the office, I felt the silent glow of peace inside my heart.

His Mysterious Ways

IN SEPTEMBER of last year, Sister Grace began forming a picture of a Christmas tree in her mind. As the director of pastoral care at Charleston's St. Francis Xavier Hospital, Sister Grace had been asked to decorate the tree that would be placed in the lobby of the Omni Hotel. The tree would have angels on it, and snowflakes—lots of snowflakes, exquisite ones crocheted by hand. By Thanksgiving Sister Grace had acquired the angels, but the snowflakes were not to be found.

On the day before Thanksgiving, Doris Hartvig was admitted to the hospital for tests. Doris detested idleness, and she was soon busy at work with needles and yarn.

"Could you do a snowflake?" one of the nuns, Sister Mary Joseph, asked her.

"I can," Doris replied. In fact, not long ago she had bought a book that described how to crochet snowflakes. They weren't easy to do, and each one required a lot of time.

With renewed hope, Sister Grace went to see Doris. She described in detail the Christmas tree she had her heart set on: a blue bow on top, angels clinging to the branches, and lacy snowflakes hanging from the boughs.

"How many snowflakes do you need?" Doris finally asked.

"We should have sixty," Sister Grace replied, "but there's no time to make that many."

Doris smiled. She reached under her bed, took out a bag of needlework, and drew out one beautiful crocheted snowflake after another—forty, fifty, over sixty of them! They were ironed, starched, and ready to be hung.

In September Doris Hartvig had felt a great urge to crochet snowflakes. Now she knew why.

—ROBERT HAWKINS, *December 1988*

The Gift of Sharing

DORIS CRANDALL

December 1980

Mama was preparing, on Christmas Eve, 1933, to bake her "hard-times fruitcake," so called because the only type of fruit it contained was prunes. But it was, to our family, an extra-special cake. My sisters—Lottie, Vivian, Estelle, and Dolly—and I sat around our kitchen table, shelling pecans for the cake.

None of us, except Mama, was enthusiastic, and I suspected her gaiety was partly put-on. "Mama," I asked, "why can't Grandma and Aunt Ella, and Aunt Fran and Uncle Hugh, and all the cousins come for Christmas like last year? We won't even have any music unless Joe comes and brings his guitar."

We wouldn't mind not having a Christmas tree, because we'd never had one, and Mama and Daddy had prepared us for the possibility of no presents; but the thought of no visitors or music really subdued us. Dolly, age five, the youngest, sobbed.

"Why'd we have to move, anyway?" she asked, sniffling. So Mama again explained her version of Dust-Bowl economics.

"When we had to give up our farm, we were lucky to find this place to rent, even if it is too far for the relatives to come. Don't worry, though." Mama reassured us. "Why, God might send us company for Christmas right out of the blue, if we believe strong enough." She began to pit the boiled prunes and mash them.

As we worked, a wind came up and whistled through the newspaper we'd stuffed into the cracks in the corners. A cold gust blasted us as Daddy entered through the back door after doing the chores at the barn. "It looks like we're in for a blue norther," he said, rubbing his hands together.

Later, Daddy built up a roaring cow-chip and mesquite fire in the potbellied stove in the living room, and we were about to get into our flannel nightgowns when someone knocked on the door. A traveler, wrapped in his bedroll, had missed the main road and stopped to ask for shelter from the storm for the night.

"Mind you," he said, when he'd had a cup of hot coffee, "I don't take charity. I work for my keep. I'm headed for California. I heard there's work to be had there."

Then Mama fixed our visitor a cozy pallet behind the stove. We girls went into our bedroom and all crawled into the same bed for warmth. "Reckon he's the one Mama said God might send out of the blue for Jesus' birthday?" I whispered.

"He must be. Who else'd be out in weather like this?" Lottie said, and Vivian and Estelle agreed. We snuggled, pondered, and slept.

At breakfast our guest sopped biscuits in gravy. "I never had a family that I remember," he said. "Can't recollect any name 'cept Gibson. You can call me Mr. Gibson if you want." He smiled, revealing gums without teeth. He seemed to have no possessions beyond his bedroll and the clothes he wore, but he pulled a large harmonica from his pants pocket and said "I've always had this. Want me to play something?"

So Mr. Gibson spent Christmas Day with us, and what a delight he was! He helped with the work, told us stories, and played all the beloved Christmas songs on his harmonica. He played by ear as we sang church hymns. After much pleading on our part, he agreed to stay one more night.

The next morning, when we awakened, Mr. Gibson was gone. I found his harmonica on the kitchen table. "Oh, Mama," I cried, "Mr. Gibson forgot his harmonica—the only thing he had."

Mama looked thoughtful. "No," she said softly. She picked it up and ran her palm over the curlicues etched in the metal sides. "I think he left it on purpose."

"Oh, I see," I said, "sort of a Christmas present. And we didn't give him anything."

"Yes, we did, honey. We gave him a family for Christmas," she said, and smiled.

We never saw Mr. Gibson again. Daddy had an ear for music and quickly learned to play the harmonica. Through the years, it brought many a joyful memory of that unforgettable Christmas when God sent us Mr. Gibson right out of the blue—a blue norther, that is—because he knew how much a man with music, who longed for a family, and a family without music, who longed for company, needed each other.

Sincerely . . .

KATHRYN SLATTERY

December 1986

oday, as I go into the closet to take down the boxes of Christmas ornaments, I find myself thinking of that gloomy day last January when I put them up there on the shelf. I see myself standing in the living room, looking about me, feeling wistful. . . .

Gone are the gumdrop-roofed gingerbread house on the sideboard and the miniature blue porcelain crèche, with its mysteriously iridescent Baby Jesus.

Gone are the boughs of evergreen, the holly sprigs, and the bunches of red berries that poked from behind every mirror and frame. Gone are the candles and the aroma of cider and pine. Gone, and missed most sorely, is that exquisite sense of anticipation, that feeling that something wonderful is about to happen.

All that remains of Christmas are a few dried needles somehow missed by the vacuum. One last cardboard box, on which I've scrawled "XMAS," waits to be closed and put away with the others crowding the closet's top shelf. And the angel—my Christmas angel.

He's a cherub, bronze, with stubby wings. I purchased him quite by chance at an auction one rainy winter afternoon. Now I look at him standing on tippy-toe, his chubby arms—so like those of our own baby boy—stretching heavenward. What is it that he sees? The wonder and mystery of our Lord's birth, I like to think.

He's quite heavy, not fragile at all. Still, as though he were made of the finest bone china, I wrap him in yards and yards of tissue and gently push him deep into the box. There he will lie until next year, snug among the children's Christmas stockings with their glue-and-glitter names, oblivious to the cycle of birthdays, holidays, and other small pleasures the coming months will bring.

Before closing the box, I take one last, lingering look around our house, and a familiar sadness washes over me. A home after Christmas, stripped of its decoration, seems barren, empty. Despite the ubiquitous clutter of papers, knickknacks, and stray toys, I sense that something is lacking. My life, it occurs to me, might be likened to our home: my life, without Christ's indwelling spirit, is barren and empty. But with Christ's spirit, it is abundant, expectant.

Suddenly, impulsively, I reach into the box and retrieve my little friend. Racing toward the living room, I set my angel on the table behind the sofa. . . .

And there, shaded by a pastel spray of silken wildflowers, he has remained, on tippy-toes, with arms and gaze upraised—a winsome reminder of the spirit of Christmas in our home this whole year long.

A Bit of Heaven on Earth

MICHAEL LANDON

December 1986

I remember very well the moment when the idea came to me. It was a Friday afternoon. I was driving home on a Los Angeles freeway through horrendous traffic. Tempers were frayed. Horns were honking. Challenges and insults were being hurled back and forth. And I found myself thinking, *Why is there so much anger everywhere? Why do people seem to despise one another? Why are they wasting all this energy on rage? If they'd use even a fraction of it on being kind, what a revolution that would be!*

And then I thought, *Why couldn't there be a television series based on the notion that kindness, not anger, is the real answer to life's problems?* That was the original seed from which *Highway to Heaven* ultimately grew.

The idea of making the central character an angel came later. Human do-gooders can become pompous or boring, but an angel can escape such labels simply by being an angel. Also, an angel can appear wherever he's wanted or needed; he's not tied to a desk or a nine-to-five job. We decided to name our angel Jonathan Smith. He wouldn't use supernatural powers to solve problems; he would persuade human beings to solve them by helping one another.

We wanted to make our angel as appealing as possible. He could feel human emotions: jealousy, for example. He could make mistakes. But he could be a spiritual catalyst in people's lives.

Most important, he could tap the fascination that angels always have had for the average person. Angels are mentioned over three hundred times in the Bible. Their best-known appearance was to herald Christ's birth, but they also play important roles in the Old Testament. An angel tells Abraham that his wife, Sarah, will have a child long after her childbearing years have ended. An angel wrestles with Jacob. Other angels warn Lot to flee the doomed city of Sodom. Many people believe that angels still appear from time to time, carry out some function helpful to humans, and then disappear as mysteriously as they came. The concept of angels is a very real part of our cultural heritage, and it seemed to me that if this concept were wedded to the notion that kindness is the answer to countless human problems, we might have an appealing basis for a TV series.

And not just appealing, but helpful. I really believe that if people are surrounded by anger and hostility, if they look for the worst and expect the worst from others, their lives are going to be stunted. If all the ideas you carry around with you are negatives, your life is going to be a negative too. Fears are magnified; failures become more threatening. Anxieties are more intense. Anger begins to dominate.

I have some serious doubts about the role of the media in all this. Most moviegoers, as everyone knows, are young people. Too many of the films designed for them are full of violence and anger; very few offer gentleness or kindness. And what's the result of this? Well, if you feed a child nothing but candy, candy is going to be what he likes and looks for, because that is all he knows. The same thing is true of violence—I believe if you fill a young mind with graphic depictions of senseless brutality, that's what the owner of the mind learns to like and enjoy. It makes it very hard for him to learn the key lesson of living—that kindness brings even greater rewards to the person who offers it than to the person who receives it.

Why am I so hung up on this business of kindness? Perhaps because it was so absent from my own childhood. My father was Jewish; my mother was Catholic. They fought constantly about everything, often in my presence, which is very hard on a child. There was no gentleness, no demonstrated affection; I developed a terrific desire to get away and build an entirely different life. I've made some mistakes along the way (who hasn't?), but it's interesting that all three of my major TV series—first *Bonanza*, then *Little House on the Prairie*, and now *Highway*—put major emphasis on family ties and family values, all reflective of what I feel.

I remember very well the incident that first made me realize what an emotional lift can come from doing an unexpected kindness for someone. I was nineteen, and I had just completed my first acting job, a very small part in a TV show called *John Nesbitt's Passing Parade*. I had $260 in my pocket, the remains of my $300 paycheck after deductions. I felt so rich and famous that I decided to go up to Beverly Hills, where I almost never went, and look in the fancy store windows.

So I did, and in front of a toy store I saw a couple of youngsters looking hungrily at items in the window. Clearly they couldn't afford to buy anything, and so—still feeling rich and famous— I asked them what they saw that they liked. One pointed to a little red wagon; the other looked yearningly at a model airplane. So I took them inside and bought them those items. Their faces were wonderful to behold, but what astonished me was the lift I got, a pleasure deeper and more satisfying than anything I had experienced before. And more lasting. As you can see, here I am telling you about it thirty years later.

Our show gave me many opportunities to observe what happens when kindness is applied to a human problem. One of our episodes dealt with child cancer victims, and we asked some real victims to read for parts. One of these kids was named Josh Wood. He had lost a leg to cancer, but what seemed to bother him more was a speech defect. He stammered so badly that he wouldn't even try to talk on the telephone. So when we asked him to read, he apologized in advance. He was sure he couldn't do it.

"Listen," I said to him, "the important thing about acting is to be a good actor. If you can be that, nothing else matters. So you stammer. So you'll be a good actor who stammers, that's all."

The kid looked at me for a long time. When we gave him the part, his stammer disappeared. Not only that, it never came back. His parents were overjoyed and amazed. All the kid needed was that little bit of reassurance from someone in a position of authority. When he got it, he was set free.

Our show helped a lot of people with problems; the mail proved that. There was one man who had been paralyzed as the result of an auto accident. He knew he would be in a wheelchair for the rest of his life, and he sank into a deep depression. He stayed in his bedroom, speaking to no one. His disability checks lay around the house; he wouldn't cash them. Then one day he happened to watch an episode from our series. When it was over, he wheeled himself out of his room. "Gather up those checks," he said to his astonished family. "I'm going to take them down and deposit them. I want to go back to college." Watching kindness in action had done something to him, you see. It changed his thinking from inertia and gloom to energy and hope. Believe me, everyone involved with the show gets a tremendous lift when that sort of thing happens.

A word of caution, perhaps, where this business of kindness is concerned: A friendly overture may not always win you an instant response. Some people are wary, some are suspicious of your motives, some—caught in the trap of a poor self-image— cannot understand why anyone should be concerned about them. Never mind. You have planted a seed. And the hope that the seed will grow, the possibility that it will grow, is reward enough.

Some people seem to have an angelic streak built into them; they are just instinctively considerate and gentle and kind. My wife, Cindy, is like that; people who meet her sense it instantly. Even animals know it; they are always finding their way to her as if they knew they could count on a friendly reception.

The Bible gives no hint that an angel might ever take the form of an animal, but to dog lovers that's not a totally inconceivable concept. In fact, we used the idea in one episode of the series. A car containing a man and his son and their dog named Boomer went out of control and rolled down the side of a ravine, coming to rest in some dense trees that hid it from view. The human passengers, both injured, were trapped inside the car. Finding them would have been almost impossible, had not a big dog kept trying to attract the attention of people in the vicinity. The dog finally succeeded in leading some rescuers to the hidden wreck in time to save the people inside. Was the dog actually Boomer? No, because Boomer had been killed in the crash and his body was still inside the car.

The impact of kindness on a sour or embittered spirit has been a favorite Christmas theme ever since Charles Dickens brought about the redemption of Scrooge in *A Christmas Carol*. A Christmas episode called "Bassinger's New York" is about a cynical newspaperman who writes a downbeat and sardonic column about life in general. He ridicules Christmas in particular. When I reveal to him that I, Jonathan Smith, am an angel, he jeers at that.

So I take Mr. Bassinger on a kind of guided tour of New York, a tour designed to melt the ice around his heart. He sees those who have little sharing what they have with others. He sees people truly caring about other people. Finally the tour brings him to a shelter where there is no more room for homeless people seeking shelter from the freezing night. And among those being turned away are a young couple. The man's name is Joseph and the woman's name is Mary, and they are expecting their first child. . . .

As Christmas approaches, why not make a promise to yourself: the promise that in the year ahead you'll be a little more openhearted in your dealings with people, a little more inclined to look for the good rather than the bad, a little more willing to assume the risks of caring—maybe just a little more angelic.

A Giant Beside Our House

RON GULLION

December 1989

I am in our yard on Big Fir Court, gazing up at the mighty 250-foot tree the street is named for. Rising from the corner of our property to the height of a twenty-story building, the great white fir dwarfs our home and everything in sight like some ancient giant. It gives the illusion of leaning ominously toward me, creaking and swaying ever so slightly in the rustling wind.

Look! It's not leaning, it's falling! It's toppling toward our house, gaining momentum, rushing to meet its shadow, until finally it crumples the roof and splinters through the living room and front bedroom with a sickening, thunderous roar. I let out a cry. Alison's room!

I awoke in a drenching sweat and sat straight up trying to blink away the terrifying vision. Another nightmare. I slipped out of bed and stole a peek into Alison's room. Our nine-year-old daughter was sleeping peacefully, as was eleven-year-old Heath across the hall. But I couldn't shake the irrational fear until I'd checked. This was not the first time I'd dreamed of such an accident. In another dream I'd seen a giant tree limb tearing loose and slamming down on Heath, leaving him crippled.

As a computer engineer, I deal with quantifiable information. I don't pay much attention to impractical things like dreams. But these nightmares were so vivid and frightening. I eased back into bed next to my wife, Nita, but not before looking out the window at the tree. There it stood, stately and still, its coarse bark ghostly pale in the faint moonlight.

A few nights later I had another dream, this one more puzzling than alarming: I am in our yard and in front of me stands a white angel. The angel has a broken wing.

What did all these dreams mean?

Then one day I noticed a twenty-foot dead limb dangling from the fir. Out here in the Northwest we call a dangerous limb like that a widow maker. I remembered the dream about Heath. "Don't go near that tree," I warned him. That Saturday I enlisted a neighbor to help me rope it down; all week I'd worried about the precarious branch. Later I had some other dead limbs removed too.

Why am I so concerned about this tree? I wondered. *It's stood here for generations. It even survived the fierce Columbus Day storm of 1962.*

My nightmares about the tree eventually subsided. Christmas season arrived, and Nita and I rushed madly to get our shopping done. More than anything, Alison wanted a Cabbage Patch doll. We scoured the stores around Portland with no luck. Everywhere we went it was the same story. "Sorry, folks," the clerk would say. "We sold out of our Cabbage Patch dolls weeks ago."

Finally Nita settled on a handmade rag doll. It was thicker and heavier than the Cabbage Patch version, but there was something about it that caught our fancy. "Well," sighed Nita as we paid for it, "this will have to do."

"Alison will love it," I reassured her.

We arrived home to a surprise. Alison had impetuously decided to rearrange her room. She'd been talking about it for days, but Nita had implored her to wait until the holiday excitement died down. "Then I'll help you," she'd promised.

Instead Alison had recruited her brother for the task, getting Heath to help drag her heavy bed across the room. "I just wanted to get it done now, Mommy," she explained as Nita surveyed the scene with obvious displeasure. "It's important." Alison's toys and furniture spilled out into the hall. By bedtime, however, Alison had her room in order again and we could scarcely hide our admiration.

"See?" said Alison knowingly. "It's not such a big deal."

Outside I heard the wind whistle through the big fir.

A howling blizzard marked Christmas Eve. I drove home from work through swirling snow and pounding winds. I pulled into the driveway, turned up my collar, and hurried inside to get ready for church. Church was not one of my priorities even under the best circumstances, and on a night like this I didn't want to be anywhere but inside my house, Christmas Eve or not. But I'd promised.

At the service with Nita and the kids, I felt strangely

detached as I hunched in the pew with my arms folded tightly, thinking about whether I even believed that God was a part of my life. I'd been raised in church but that was a long time ago. Now I certainly didn't feel any "tidings of comfort and joy." God may have created the world and all its wonders, but I didn't see where that had much to do with my life. If God was real, he was much too remote for me to have faith in him.

We arrived home late, and the wind and snow stung our faces as we walked up the driveway. Heath and Alison rushed inside to turn on the Christmas tree lights. From our bay window the blue lights cast a peaceful glow across the snowy yard. I draped my arm around Nita and led her in.

Wrapping paper flew as the children tore into their presents, and Nita and I settled back on the couch to view the happy chaos. Nita had turned the tree into a work of art. The crowning touch was a glorious blond angel perched high at the top. "It looks like Alison," I said.

Alison was so delighted with her big new doll that she granted it the honor of accompanying her to bed. "Told you she'd love it," I reminded Nita as we climbed under the covers. The moaning wind lulled us to sleep.

Roar! The explosive sound jolted the house. I hadn't been asleep long, and my startled, half-awake mind tried to separate fantasy from reality. *The dream again*, I thought. But then I sat bolt upright, and suddenly I knew. This was no dream. This time my nightmare was real. The tree really had fallen on our house!

I leapt out of bed and raced across the hall to Alison's room. "Daddy, help!" she was calling frantically. "I'm stuck!"

I couldn't budge the door. It was jammed shut. "Oh, my God," I whispered. "Don't move, honey!" I shouted through the door. "We'll get you out." I grabbed a flashlight and told Nita to call 911. "I'll see if I can get to her from outside."

I was horrified to find the tree filling the front hall, branches whipping in the gale. I stumbled through the family room to a side door. Outside I nearly collided with the massive trunk. Propped up on its giant ball of roots, which had been torn from the earth, it looked prehistoric. I crawled underneath as the rough bark tore at my robe and ripped my flesh. The wind sliced through me. Above the din I heard the distant wail of sirens.

Groping my way to Alison's window, I aimed the flashlight beam inside and wiped the icy snow from my eyes. All I could see were branches, tattered insulation, and hunks of ceiling strewn about the trunk. Somewhere buried beneath the tree was my daughter, crying faintly, "Daddy! Daddy!"

Someone was standing beside me. "Alison! This is Captain McCullough of the fire department," he called. "Your daddy's with me. Can you move at all?"

"I think I can move my arm," came a brave little voice.

"Good. Push your hand up as high as you can."

Tiny fingers wriggled up through the debris. I breathed a tentative sigh of relief. Firemen rushed to set up lights and heat lamps. They fastened a plastic tarp over the rescue area. Captain McCullough turned to me and said quietly, "This isn't going to be easy, Mr. Gullion."

As I huddled with Nita, and neighbors looked after Heath, a terrifying game of pick-up sticks slowly unfolded. The night air was filled with the roar of chain saws and the reek of fir pitch as rescuers cut away at the tree and cautiously removed branches as they went. A slight shift of any debris could spell disaster.

Bit by bit they chipped away at the wreckage until, after an hour, Alison's head and shoulders emerged. Her right leg appeared to be crushed under the tree. A fallen two-by-six rafter clamped down on her torso. We could see Alison's new doll squeezed between her chest and the rafter. Apparently she'd fallen asleep clutching it.

McCullough shook his head grimly and called a halt to the work. "We can't risk it," he said. "Show me the crawlspace." Moments later he played his flashlight on the area under Alison's room. Limbs a half foot in diameter pierced the floor and stabbed the ground beneath. Again McCullough shook his head. "We can't cut away the floor without disturbing the tree. And that tree must not shift."

The subzero wind had intensified. Hours had passed and now there was the threat of Alison succumbing to hypothermia. Neighbors rushed in warm blankets and hot-water bottles. A paramedic put his wool ski cap on Alison's head. But I could see she was drifting, her big eyes fluttering. Once or twice her head rolled back. If we didn't get her leg out soon, the surgeons might have to amputate it to free her.

Only one chance was left: lift the tree. A crane was out of the question. In this wind it would be too unstable. But McCullough had called a towing company that used giant air bags to gently right overturned semitrailers. "It's a gamble," he warned me. "But we've run out of options."

Huge rubber bags were packed under the tree. A compressor roared to life. Slowly the bags filled with air and swelled against the great fir. Despite the blizzard, I could see sweat bead up on McCullough's tensed brow. My hands trembled as Nita buried her head in my chest, afraid to look.

Suddenly I heard myself praying to the God whose very existence, just hours earlier, I'd doubted. You would have thought I'd be ashamed to ask his help now, but something told me I must. "Please, Lord," I begged, "spare her life. I believe you are there."

The shriek of the compressor was deafening. The bags bulged like great billows, but at first nothing gave.

Then there was movement! Inch by agonizing inch, the tree was lifted. A cry rose from the crowd as paramedics rushed to free Alison and whisk her to a waiting ambulance. Nita and I jumped in with her, and we roared off. Alison smiled weakly. "I'll be okay now, Daddy," she whispered, still grasping her new doll.

That overstuffed doll, it turned out, was possibly just enough of a cushion between the fallen two-by-six rafter and Alison's chest to have saved her life.

The doctors confirmed that she would recover. And Alison's leg was only broken, not crushed.

Christmas Day, Heath and I kicked through the rubble of our house. I'd been thinking about that desperate prayer I'd said, thinking about it a lot. In Alison's room I saw that the bulk of the fir had landed near the southeast wall—right where her bed had been before she'd impulsively moved it. On the trunk directly over where Alison lay when the tree came crashing through, I noticed a wide scar from a recently cut branch—one of those I'd felt such urgency to remove after my dream. That branch might have killed her.

Had God been trying to warn me all along about the tree? To protect us? Had I been blind to God's ways?

In the snow, outside what used to be our living room, I found the angel from our Christmas tree, the one that looked like Alison. Its wing was broken, just as the angel's wing in my dream had been. As I brushed it off and held it up, Heath came running. "Dad, Dad!" He grabbed the angel. "I've seen this before! In a dream! An angel with a broken wing just like this one!"

Dreams—does God speak to us through them? The Bible says he does, as well as in many other ways. This much I myself can say: Alison is safe and well. And God is, and always has been, watching over my family.

"A Whirling Above My Head"

MARJORIE MARTIN

December 1994

L
ast Christmas Eve, Dr. Norman Vincent Peale, pastor of
Marble Collegiate Church for more than fifty years and
cofounder and first editor of *Guideposts*, died at the age of ninety-
five. In the weeks following, his wife, Ruth Stafford Peale,
received this letter from a member of the Marble congregation.

> Dear Mrs. Peale,
>
> On Christmas Eve, after a lovely evening with family
> members, I'd started to fall asleep when there was a
> great whirling above my head. Thousands of angels
> appeared—all bright and shining and exulting—
> crowded together, singing alleluias in glorious voices.
> Everything, even the sound, was filled with colors that
> were incredibly loud and full and rich. I should have
> been frightened, but instead I felt the way a child does
> when something impossibly wonderful has happened.

It was as if I were standing on a mountaintop as this huge throng of exulting angels filled the sky. My eyes were open and I could see the windows of my bedroom, but the multitude of angels floated over it, and the music was a massive, gorgeous roar of praise. I thought I must have a raging fever and must be dying—but it didn't matter because I felt at the center of life.

This lasted until seven A.M., when my alarm went off. Even then, as I sat up in bed, I could still hear and see the angels more vividly than the world around me. I thought I would be exhausted from the lack of sleep, but as I stepped out of bed I felt exhilarated, joyful, complete. Later that night I heard on the news that Norman Vincent Peale had passed on. Immediately it all made sense! I think I was in on the heavenly celebration for Dr. Peale's arrival.

On December 29 I attended Dr. Peale's memorial service. Mrs. Peale, when you said, "I believe Norman is having a great time with the angels up there," I was overwhelmed. I simply had to write and share my own remarkable experience.

Serenade at Sunrise

JANICE BROOKS-HEADRICK

December 1996

I had never been more homesick or stressed than that Christmas in 1981, the year my husband, Charles, and I pulled up stakes and moved to the Texas badlands to work in the vast oil fields of the panhandle. We were thousands of miles away from home for the first time. Our relationship was young, so we didn't have the comfort of long years of habit to smooth over the lumps in life. Money was tight. If I hadn't been madly in love with the man with the turquoise-blue eyes, I would have run home to Mama. As it was, I cried every time I heard "White Christmas."

Texas just didn't look right—nineteen shades of brown, flat, and nary a tree in sight. Charles and I were both mountain-born and raised back east, in Tennessee and upstate New York respectively. Out in the badlands—with no green hills to hold me in their hollows—I felt as if I might fall off the earth.

Charles had three children from a previous marriage who

came along to live with us—Charlie, fifteen, Sherri, fourteen, and Kresti, nine. All were sick for a full three months after the move—measles, chicken pox, tonsillitis. They grew out of clothes faster than they grew into them. Then there was Charles's brother Jim. A gifted musician, Jim had rolled through from the West Coast on his way to Nashville. He stopped in the café where I waited tables and said he would be in town for a few days, sleeping in his car. I offered him our couch. Four months later, Jim was still on the couch.

With six mouths to feed, house and car payments, doctor bills and what have you, we worked countless hours just to make ends meet. One night I woke up crying. I didn't know how to work any harder, any smarter, or make any more money to afford a good old Christmas like back home. This year we just wouldn't have Christmas. It broke my heart.

Not long after, Jim came in from his job at a shop where he repaired drilling equipment to say there was a fellow who needed his wells watched during Christmas. Wells have to be watched when workers aren't around, and they would all be off for the holiday. If the generators go on the blink, the wells can explode. Besides, this fellow had had some tools and expensive equipment turn up missing and he suspected thieves had been sneaking around.

Charles, Jim and I had a quick conference around the kitchen table. "If we take the work," Charles said, "we can afford to celebrate a few days early. Then we'll watch the wells in shifts on Christmas Eve and Christmas, with one of us always here to keep an eye on the kids."

That's how I came to be guarding an oil well my first Christmas Eve in Texas.

Charles's job was to baby-sit the gas well. It needed a practiced eye because gas wells can blow sky-high if anything goes wrong. Jim and I split shifts at the big oil well. He drove me out for my shift with the kids and my feisty keeshond, Foxy, crammed in the backseat. I had been told there was a trailer with phone, electricity, radio, TV, and flush toilets. Still I was nervous. That's why I was bringing Foxy along, as well as the .22 in my purse. I was worried about those thieves. We were jouncing along when Charlie hollered, "Look!"

In the black-velvet sky shone a single dazzling star. Yes, like everything else in Texas, stars are big But I had never seen anything like the brilliance of that star in the eastern sky. It was the size of my fist. "You think that's the same star the Wise Men saw?" Charlie wondered aloud. For an instant it really felt like Christmas.

My joy faded, though, when we bounced into the oil well site. It's hard to convey the size, smell and roar of a Texas oil rig. The drilling floor was almost five stories off the ground! Jim went over the checklist with me for the monstrous generators. Set inside a building, they reeked of fuel and made a noise like their name: Waukeshaws. *Wa-kee-sha . . . wa-kee-sha . . .* Despite the bulky ear protectors I wore, the noise still drummed into my bones.

A vast waste pit contained drainage from the rig. The stench of oil permeated everything. It was about as far from the Norman Rockwell Christmas of my dreams as I could have imagined.

Jim dropped me and Foxy off at the trailer. "See you tomorrow," he said as he and the kids drove off. "Merry Christmas!"

I tried to settle in. I had brought some sewing to do and some snacks. I turned on the TV but reception was bad this far from a transmitter. I thought of my relatives back in Tennessee—cousins, brothers, sisters, nephews, uncles, aunts—all having a joyous Christmas Eve together. I grabbed the phone, thinking to call my folks in New York. *At least we can cry together*, I told myself. The phone was dead.

I hoped robbers wouldn't be out on Christmas Eve. I had Foxy, who would bristle, snarl and snap if there was trouble, though I didn't think she had it in her to attack. Well, I could shoot the thieves—if I had it in me. I checked the pistol. It had no bullets. *Great.* I was thirty miles from help, with no car, a phone that didn't work, a dog that wouldn't bite, and a gun that couldn't shoot. *Lord*, I prayed, *please don't forget about me all alone out here.*

It was a good thing I had brought the sewing. The generators wouldn't need checking until morning. I sewed until my eyelids got heavy, then bundled up and went to sleep.

I awoke to dawn drifting in the windows. Sunrise in the desert is wondrous, the colors amplified by the stark landscape. Texans say when God was making the world he ran out of mountains, trees and rivers by the time he got to the Texas badlands. So he just emptied his paint box and gave them the most glorious sunsets and sunrises on earth. I think it takes that kind of desolation to make room for so much beauty.

As a bonus, my favorite Christmas hymn, "Joy to the

World!" was playing on the radio. Smiling sleepily, I reached to turn it up and was quite surprised I couldn't. The radio wasn't playing. It wasn't even plugged in.

"He rules the world . . ."

It sounded like a huge choir, the soaring voices blending perfectly. I looked at the TV. It too was off. I got up and unplugged it anyway. Still the choir rang out, even over the thrum of the Waukeshaws. It seemed like the sound was coming from everywhere at once.

"And makes the nations prove . . ."

I searched the trailer. There was no radio, no TV, no tape player to account for the ringing chorus of joyous voices. I knew the song by heart and could understand every word the choir sang. Sound carries far in the desert, but thirty miles? Impossible. It must be coming from outside.

I wrapped my coat around me and stepped out into the sharp morning air. Foxy was dancing circles around my ankles, her ears at the alert. We looked and looked for a source. The music seemed to be coming from the east . . . from all of the east.

"No more let sins and sorrows grow . . ."

Was there someone on the other side of the pit? Jim blasting the car radio to wake me up? Foxy and I climbed an embankment. We were completely alone with the most awesome sunrise I had ever seen, even for Texas. The midnight-blue of the sky lightened into vivid colors that spilled across the desert—lilac, cerulean, magenta, sienna.

I sat on the cold, sandy bank, my arm around Foxy, awash with music and light. There were no other intrusions on my senses—no sounds, no smells. Maybe I was hallucinating. Maybe I was reacting to stress and loneliness. When the verses were over, no doubt, the music would fade. But then something happened, something I still can't explain.

The voices swelled into a fourth verse of "Joy to the World!" I knew only three verses. Still, I was hearing a fourth as clear as the day that was dawning, with the full force of the invisible cosmic serenade. I cannot remember the words to that verse. They were rich with praise and glory, I know, and clear to me at the time. But today I cannot repeat a single line. (I've checked hymn books and discovered a fourth verse—though not the one I heard that morning!) Like the colors of that dawn sky, the words were both tangible and intangible, meant only for the moment yet leaving an impression for a lifetime.

A heavenly host sang that morning out in a Texas oil field. I thought I was alone and forgotten, forced to endure the most desolate Christmas of my life. But God shook me awake with an unforgettable reminder that his glory and the glory of his Son are ever-present.

Author Index

Date Index

NORMAN VINCENT PEALE had a genius for discerning the power in a good idea. When his friend Raymond Thornburg came to him in 1945 with the idea of an inspirational newsletter for businessmen, Dr. Peale sensed immediately that there was an important need to be filled. By that February, the concept had evolved into *Guideposts* magazine.

Guideposts' theme was clear from the single article in that first issue: "I Believe in Prayer" by war hero Captain Eddie Rickenbacker. This magazine would be a place where people from all walks of life—movie stars, business executives, athletes, teachers, housewives, and war heroes—talked about their faith.

The little magazine struggled but subscriptions increased. Then a fire destroyed the magazine's subscriber list. The famous broadcaster Lowell Thomas spoke on his radio show of what had happened to the fledgling publication. The result? *Guideposts* gained even more subscribers than before.

Right from the beginning, readers not only sent in their stories but also their requests for prayer. The staff started to gather regularly on Monday mornings, sharing the requests and praying for readers. The staff also turned to its supporters for inspiration. When financial setbacks threatened to overwhelm the magazine, an early backer accused the staff of thinking *lack*. "Visualize success and you will have it," she said. Positive thinking won the day.

New magazines were added to the Guideposts family: *Angels on Earth*, in 1995; *Sweet 16*, a magazine for teen girls; and, most recently, *Positive Thinking* (www.positivethinkingmag.com). And those prayer requests that used to come by mail now come in the tens of thousands via the Internet. But the purpose of the organization has never changed.

"Find a need and fill it," was how Dr. Peale would put it. That's been the secret of *Guideposts'* success year after year.